Velvet Bonds

THE CHINESE FAMILY

Michael Saso

New Life Center

CARMEL, CALIFORNIA

ISBN 1–929431–00-7

Camera-ready copy was prepared by the author.

This book was printed on acid-free paper and meets the
guidelines for permanence and durability of the Council on
Library Resources.

Printed by Data Reproductions Corporation

Distributed by
University of Hawai'i Press
2840 Kolowalu Street
Honolulu, Hawai'i 96822

DEDICATION

To all of the families who provided the lively acccounts of chapters 3 and 4, especially the matriarchs of Luguhu on the Tibet-Yunnan border, for whom youth and elderly are equally cherished, and benevolence is a way of life.

CONTENTS

ILLUSTRATIONS

(*Photos by Alden Stevenson, S.J.)

ACKNOWLEDGMENTS

The author wishes to express heartfelt thanks to Nariko Akimoto for the immense amount of help and analysis that went into writing chapters 5 and 6; to Susan Moriyama and Lin Yüeh-ch'in for the charts and analysis of chapter 7; Zhang Xiu for the moving stories of chapter 3; and the Muosuo, Aini, Amdo nomads, and Qinghai Hui for the family histories provided in chapter 4. Studies on the Chinese family published after 1986 are not adequately accounted for, due to the isolation from library and bookstore sources imposed by Tibetan highlands and other inaccessible places. The title *Velvet Bonds* was suggested by Patrick Dowdey. The photos were taken by Alden Stevenson, S.J. The woodblock prints are from fragments found in secondhand Taipei bookshops, remnants of Japanese who were enchanted by Taiwan in the 1920's and 1930's. Lucille Aono worked long hours to help edit the final copy, and Robert Campbell gave expert advice in making the text and layout more readable. All omissions and mistakes are solely my own.

Michael Saso
Yuanmingyuan Donglu
Beijing, June, 1998

INTRODUCTION

Velvet Bonds, a study that began in the fall of 1972, and came to a conclusion in the summer of 1998, affirms with certainty and clarity that the family is the core and center of Chinese social and cultural life. Within its embrace are worked out rites of passage, seasonal festivities, and basic economic survival. Without a family of some sort or other, one can only survive as an "outsider," on the fringes of Chinese society.

My first experience of family life in China began in August, 1955, after a two week voyage on the "Sally Maersk," a Danish freighter bound for Asia. We skirted two typhoons and witnessed the flaming sunsets of the San Bernardino straits in the Philippines before landing in the bustling port of Keelung, north Taiwan. No one was there to meet us, so our first day in China was spent with the friendly customs official, who took us to lunch while someone was contacted to come and get us.

Because the new language school of Fu Jen University in the nearby city of Hsinchu was not yet completed, we were bused with other aspiring students of Chinese language to a farming village called Kuanhsi (Guanxi: West Pass), nestled against the tea growing hills of Hsinchu county. There we were housed for two months with a farmer's family, in a mud-brick home surrounded by rice paddy, vegetable gardens, and lush green hills. Here we learned our first words of Mandarin Chinese on a stamped earth floor, in an adobe brick, walled home of a Hakka Chinese farming family.

Standard Chinese (Mandarin) was not the language of the Hakka speaking farming families of Kuanhsi, nor of the Fukien merchants of Hsinchu city, who spoke another dialect called *Minnan-hua.* Though Minnan and Hakka dialects were quite different, almost everyone could use an accented form of broken mandarin. We students beginning the study of Mandarin Chinese could distinguish the clear "r" sounds of our Beijing teachers from the flat "sz" and "dz" equivalents of southern mandarin. The Hakka thought that we and our teachers were all strangers, foreigners to the culture of south China. The linguisic differences hinted of deeper cultural and socal differences between the provinces of north, central, and south China.

Our first words of Chinese were spoken within the four walls of an extended Hakka farming family. In the compound where we lived were three generations. Grandparents were in a central room, surrounded by children and grandchildren's households, all connected by roofs and courtyards in a grand, traditional family residence.

After this idyllic introduction to Chinese family life, we were moved into the city of Hsinchu when the language school was completed. Our daily lives were lived in equally close proximity to the families of that conservative city, who spoke the Minnan dialect from southern Fukien province. Hsinchu was known for its scholars, traditional ways, and a suburban scientific community who taught in two famous universities.

Instead of connected single story rooms, city families lived in dwellings which were built upwards, in two or three story high residences. Households were equally large, focused on grandparents, parents, and children's well-being and livelihood. Each extended household residence, whether in the rural countryside or the crowded city, was centered around a family altar with an ancestor tablet and spirit shrine, and a kitchen stove around which the entire family gathered for meals.

Whether Hakka farmer or Minnan merchant, each morning the grandmother, or some senior female person of the family, lit incense and offered food, water, and wine to the spirits and ancestors commemorated on the family altar. Our mandarin teachers from north China, we noted, did not do this.

The hearth, where family meals were cooked and often eaten, was the focal point of Hakka and Minnan family life. The fancy table in the front room by the family altar was reserved for festival days and important guests, such as we foreign language students when invited for dinner, or a visit.

Our language teachers from Beijing, whose northern accent we were told to emulate, did not claim to understand or relate to the temple rituals or family customs of the Hakka and Minnan-speaking peoples of Hsinchu. Not only accents, but also life styles were significantly different.

It was obvious that the culture of greater China was not the exclusive property of any province or linguistic group. Language and accent carried ritual and festival variations, seen not only in dinners and casual home visits, but also in celebrations observed in Taoist and Buddhist temples, weddings and funerals, even in simple everyday events.

An interesting example of this happened soon after our arrival in the Hakka farming village. It was the twenty-eighth day of the Seventh Lunar Month, (fourteen days after "All Souls Day," the full moon festival of the Seventh Lunar month). Each Hakka family in the village slaughtered a pig, and laid it out on a wood frame in front of the family residence. A huge pineapple was put in the mouth of the slaughtered pig, and blinking Christmas trees lights were put in the eyes. Tables of cooked foods, drink, flowers, and fruit were laid on the tables. Taoist priests, *Tao-shih* (*Daoshr*), dressed in red silk brocade robes trimmed in green, with black skull caps and a small a gold crown, stopped in front of each house and chanted prayers.

The next morning when our Mandarin teachers from Beijing came to teach us, none of them could explain what the festival was, the meaning of the Taoist robes, or the sacrifice of a whole hog. Life was much better in Beijing than in Taiwan, they assured us. Temples were bigger, festivals more colorful, and life much more Chinese. Taiwan was closer to Africa than Beijing in its customs, one of our Beijing born-and-raised teachers jokingly told us.

The next day, our teachers found a learned answer to our query. The celebration for releasing souls from hell, called *P'u-tu* (*pudu*) in Taiwan, *Kuei-chieh* (*guijie*) in Beijing, was a festivity observed throughout China on the fifteenth day of the Seventh Lunar month. Translated "Ghost festival," it was the day on which the gates of Hell were opened, and the suffering souls in the underworld released. It was similar to Halloween, or "All Souls Day" in the west.

Fourteen days after the fifteenth, (the twenty-eighth of the Seventh Lunar Month) the gates of hell were closed again, and the freed souls sent back to the underworld. This "closing of hell," especially colorful in the Hakka areas of Hsinchu County, was what we had seen. It commemorated all those killed in the wars of the mid-nineteenth century, when Hakka were slaughtered by Minnan settlers, coinciding with the "Taiping" Hakka rebellion in central China.

In spite of obvious differences, such as festivals, house structure, and language, there were other, very definite things, that Minnan and Hakka Chinese had in common with the mainlanders from other parts of China. The first was an intense loyalty to being Chinese, an awareness of Chinese national and cultural identity as distinct from people who were not ethnically Chinese, i.e., we foreigners and the aborigines of the highlands.

The second was the reliance on a life-long bond to the family. Family ties were universal. Both unyielding and yet soft, family ties were like *velvet bonds*, a universal principle binding the nuclear, extended, and clan family together. The one thing that northern and southern Chinese felt in common was a sense of warmth, obligation and at the same time overwhelming burden of the family.

Even though all other things, such as rituals in Chinese temples, market food supplies, local and familial customs were different for each village, county, and province of China, all felt some common bond that made them "Chinese." The focus of life for all, Hakka farmers, Minnan merchants, and mainland teachers from the north all assured us, something that all shared in common were the velvet bonds that chained one eternally to the family. At least in the sense of shared values, expressed in explicit written Chinese characters such as filiality (*xiao*), reciprocal obligation (*yi*), and respect (*li*) our teachers and farming family hosts held something in common.

The very first time that I felt a deep, impelling desire to write something about the Chinese family occurred shortly after our move into Hsinchu city. The language school had been erected on *Nan-ta lu (Nandalu* Great South Road), across the railroad tracks, in a mixed Hakka-Minnan neighborhood.

Each morning, before sunrise, street sellers came by our windows, selling *Do-a* (Taiwanese for tofu, fresh bean curd), sweet peanut soup ("meedee" in local dialect), and *yu-t'iao* (deep-fried foot-long donut sticks) which the seller called *yujiagui-yo* (a demon deep fried in oil). I turned on my tape-recorder, reserved for language study, and made a recording of the street sellers' words.

That day in class, I asked our Mandarin teachers what the words in the recording meant. They, of course, did not know. The difficulties of learning Minnan dialect and customs lay beyond their range of interests.

That evening when the neighborhood children came home from school, I played the recording again, from my window that opened out into the neighborhood alley. Immediately I was beset by elementary school children, hearing recorded street-sellers for the first time. My recording was a neighborhood sensation. I soon found out that the word *yujiagui-you* was a Taiwan and southern Fujian province pun; "fried demon" referred to the evil official who had killed the folk hero Yue Fei, a late Song dynasty (960-1281) hero. Everyone knew who the fried demon was, except for our Mandarin teachers (who begrudgingly admitted that the word was used in Beijing and throughout north of China too).

The child who explained all this to me was a nine-year-old girl student named Fu Meiliang (Fu Beautiful Light). I asked which of the many doorways and households on the street was her home. She pointed to one, but did not say "it's my home," or any other term of identification. The other children said teasingly "*simpua*" (Mandarin: *t'ung-yang hsi, (tongyangxi)*, an adopted child brought up to be a bride in the family).

I did not know, of course, what *simpua* or *tongyangxi* was, at that time, after only three months of mandarin. I asked our mandarin teachers what the term meant. They, for once, were able to respond. "*Tongyangxi* are found throughout China," they all agreed. It was a common practice that poorer farming families would adopt out a girl to be a bride in another family when she grew up.

I determined at once that I should do more research and write an article for publication on this topic, and was immediately scolded by the director of the language school. "Wait until you've been here for ten years, before pretending to know anything about China," he told me. It is now forty-three years later, as I write this introduction to the study of the Chinese family.

To be called a *Zhongguo tong*, (a person who understands China), he said, was a polite way of being told that no one really knows anything about China, not the Chinese or the foreign experts who write volumes about what boils down to personal experience and anecdotal verification of statistics. Demurring from this unwanted praise, best reply that we are "*Zhongguo fantong*," people fond of Chinese cooking, who know nothing more than the anecdotal.

I have therefore divided my study into two sections, the anecdotal (chs. 2-4) and the statistical (chs. 5-7), which demonstrates, if nothing else, that statistics come to life when verified by the retelling of the events of real life.

A year from the day that I met Meiliang, she introduced her real mother to me. A Hakka woman from the same farming village near Kuanhsi (Guanxi) where we had first lived, her mother had decided to dissolve the *tongyangxi* contract with the Hsinchu family, and bring Meiliang back to their home in Kuanhsi. I asked her why the decision was made to bring their daughter back to her real home.

"We were very poor, when we first adopted her out to a family in Hsinchu," the mother told me, quite honestly. "Now we have become more affluent, in Taiwan's new economy. Besides, Meiliang wanted to return home to her own parents." Meiliang gave me a hug, then took her mother's hand, and went away. I never saw them again, after that day.

Friends of those first days in Hsinchu, students in high school or college, were my original motivation for writing about the Chinese family. In the intervening forty-odd years, they married, had children, and built their own grand households. Unlike mainland China where the police restrict foreigners in special ghettoes with controlled access to Chinese nationals, in Taiwan it is possible to live in Chinese homes.

I lived at various times in a Taoist household with my two children, with families of former students, in village temples and farming households, and in a dorm with Chinese students. Daily life in a Chinese family, seeing the expression of affection and love, quarrels and disagreements between parents and children, even animosity and trauma in family hardships and tribulations, were important elements in piecing together a fuller portrait of family life in China as seen from the hearthside, along with an exhaustive reading of learned books.

Scholars and friends who read the earlier segments of the work, that is, the statistics derived from Taiwan (1955-1974), warned that Hsinchu was by no means representative of all China. Their words were proven true again and again during my twelve year residency in mainland China between 1986-98. Modern and traditional Chinese family values as I had seen them in Hsinchu were not an adequate preparation for living in the infinitely more complicated family and political life of greater China.

To understand the role of the family in China after violent social disruption, it was essential to live and observe at first hand how much, if at all, the Chinese family had changed after 1949. I decided to retire from university teaching, and returned in 1990 to live in North and West China as I had done for so many years in Taiwan and Southeast Asia. By so doing, I could study families and daily family life in many diverse parts of modern mainland China.

The ethnic composition of greater China is overwhelming and enriching. It was very clear and evident, from the very first days of living in Beijing and other parts of north, west, and southwest China, that the lives of China's minority people were also centered, in an analogous way, on the family. The nomads of Tibet, the Muosuo matriarchy of the Yunnan-Sichuan border, the Hani-Aini of the Yunnan-Burma border, Uighur and Mongol families of the northwest lived in a manner analogously close and yet significantly different from the Han Chinese of Taiwan and southeast China.

The common element of successful livelihood in China, was the obvious fact that the family is the center and core of Han and Minority Chinese economic, social and cultural life. This is the first, strongest, and longest-lasting impression of observing the family and its role in modern China. *Family of some form or other is basic for survival in China.*

1) *Other Statistical and Anecdotal Studies of the Family*

Studies of the rural Chinese family undertaken by Arthur Wolf and Huang Chieh-shan in the Taipei basin of north Taiwan, were a stimulus and guide for my own and many others research. The methods used by Arthur Wolf to analyze household registers are adapted here in chapters 5-7.

The complementary work of Margery Wolf has been a guide for many scholars in the study of women in China. She has inspired a generation of younger students to continue the search for an adequate and meaningful presentation of the intimacies of family life through the discipline of women's studies, as well as from anthropological perspectives.

The work of Wolf and Huang remains a hallmark model for understanding the family in China. Many noted scholars, including Sophie Sa, Myron Cohen, Burton Pasternak, Maurice Freedman, Hugh Baker, and Steve Harrell, participated in the debates initiated by Arthur Wolf on the nature of marriage, adoption, kinship, and the family in China. The debate polarized around the thinking of Arthur Wolf and the statistic oriented school of American cultural anthropology, and the kinship studies of the social anthropologist Maurice Freedman of London University's School of Economics and the School of Oriental and African Studies.

Following the debates of the seventies, which were cut short by the untimely death of Maurice Freedman (who had been a mentor at London University during my own doctoral work there), John Engle's *Marriage in the People's Republic of China*, and William Parish's *Village and Family in Contemporary China* extended the analysis of the modern Chinese family to the People's Republic. Fred Blake's sensitive study, *Ethnic Groups and Social Change in a Chinese Market Town,* treats of Hakka families in the New Territories of Hongkong.

A number of conferences and publications on the Chinese family followed during the 1980's, including the work of Margery Wolf entitled *Revolution Postponed* and the published papers of the conference on *Marriage and Inequality in Chinese Society*, sponsored by the Social Science Research Council in January, 1988. (The conference papers were edited and published by Patricia Ebrey and Rubie Watson, Berkeley: University of California Press, 1991).

Fei Xiaotong, China's first and most renowned anthropologist, is known for his important contributions in analyzing Chinese society. Professor Fei's works parallel those of Chie Nakane and Niida Noboru in Japan, in describing from the intellectual's viewpoint the values and structure of the Chinese family.

Studies of the change in traditional Chinese family values were conducted by a team of scholars in America, between 1987 and 1990. Godwin Chu (East-West Center, Hawaii) published the results of a questionnaire distributed to 2,000 Chinese in the Shanghai area in 1987. In this study (*The Great Wall in Ruins*) it was found that family social values had changed significantly after the Cultural Revolution.

2) *The "Velvet Bonds" Project*
With funding from the National Science Foundation, the fall of 1972 was spent microfilming 20,000 household registers, and the following years, 1973-74, the statistical analysis of these rich sources of urban family structure was begun. The project moved to the University of Hawaii in 1974. 1974-1980 was spent writing and reworking the first version of chapters 5-7. Our statistics, charts, and family histories, were compared to Japanese and western studies of China. I was assisted at first by Nariko Akimoto, who formulated the statistics of chapter 6.

Without the knowledge garnered from the Taiwan registers, it would have been impossible to conduct the study of mainland Chinese families during the past twelve years of residency in modern China. The years 1990-98 were spent mainly with families in Beijing, Gansu, Qinghai, Yunnan and Tibet. I hoped in this segment of the work to understand the immense cultural and physical differences in lesser known parts of China. The deep attachment of all my informants to their extended families showed that throughout China, minority as well as majority, family is the center of social and cultural life.

I hope that in telling their stories, the reader may cherish and enjoy the family encounter, as I did. To the dedicated researchers, who were instrumental in bringing this work to a conclusion, must be given credit for whatever is of interest in the following pages. For faults found by reviewers, overlooking the studies of colleagues, the blame is totally mine. For all who helped so much in completing the project, I am deeply grateful and eternally indebted.

1. THE CHINESE FAMILY
(Wade-Giles romanization with text, Pinyin in parenthesis)

The ideal Chinese Family supports three generations, parents, children, and grandparents, living under one roof. All should work towards this ideal. (Chinese Academy of Social Sciences, conference report, June, `95)

In this first chapter we would like to present for the reader what modern Chinese, as well as foreign research scholars, say about the Chinese family. In effect we can say that most Chinese say very similar things about the family, when asked to define what it is, and its role in modern society. The difference between them and the foreign scholar, however, can be very great. For this reason we also present here prominent foreign scholars' views of the nature and role of the family in Chinese life.

1) *The Official (State Approved) View*
While strolling through a recent archeological display in the Palace Museum (Gugong) in Beijing guests were treated to the following report:

From the beginning of recorded Chinese civilization until today, scholars tell us, the family has always played a central role in the social, cultural, and festive life of China....Ancient heroes of the mythical past, who symbolize the importance of traditional family values, were honored from earlier times than previously believed. Sites relating to the legendary Hsia (Xia) kingdom, dating from ca. 2,300 BC, and the reign of the three rulers Yao, Shun and Yu which preceded that period were found in Szechuan, west China." (*Palace Museum exhibit*, press release, 1995).

These artifacts indicated, the newspaper report stated, a highly developed civilization predating the Hsia dynasty (ca. 2300 B.C.). Three bronze statues found on the site were identified with the three ancient sage rulers Yao, Shun, and Yu. Confucius (+481 BC), China's great sage who taught the centrality of family and its values, chose these

1

three ancient heroes as models of family life and social virtue, and therefore appointed by heaven's mandate to be rulers of the Central Kingdom. From Confucius' time until today, the government article stated, *the importance of family values in China has not diminished.*

Modern Chinese scholars, with the support of State publishers and sanction of party leaders, proclaim the family to be a basic reason for the continuing survival and vitality of Chinese civilization during the process of modernization and economic reform. In the words of a CASS (Chinese Academy of Social Science) scholar:

> The family is a source of constancy and endurance in a time of rapid economic growth and unruly social change. In spite of industrialization, socialization, and a cultural revolution that effaced any sense of pride in the traditional past, the people of China survive the tumult of economic convulsion and the primacy of implacable consumer values because the family continues to be the source of stability and strength in Chinese social life. (Conference report, CASS, Beijing, 1995).

Modern scholars in China are consistent in affirming that *the family constitutes a stable factor for social, cultural, and economic well-being in modern China.* They point to the fact that basic family values have survived the past 200 years of violent foreign and internal conflict, grueling political changes, and unexplained policy reversals. "The family," according to official news reports and other government sources, "provides a balanced and judicious role in times of personal and social crisis."

This truth is most evident in the context of modern Beijing, where "economic profit and progress" dominate every conversation and official news report in the Chinese and English press. Family stability and the education of children, on the other hand, (as the evidence in chapters 2-4 overwhelmingly shows), takes precedence over other interests when at home, away from the marketplace.

In the past, Western and Chinese scholars agree, the uniquely resilient culture of China absorbed all conquerors into its culturally nourishing system. Like butter churned from raw milk, or clay turned on the potter's wheel, to be fired in the kilns of Confucian, Buddhist and Taoist values, China's perennial culture influenced border peoples,

2

Hun, Mongol, and Manchu invaders, Korean, Japanese, and southeast Asian neighbors. East and Southeast Asia were influenced at many levels by its political and cultural cultural system.

For centuries China remained unchanged in this essentially conservative position. Its emperors received tribute from neighboring nations, while providing in return Confucian ideals for family, friendship, spiritual cultivation, and cultural values for all of Asia. China gave itself the name *Chung-kuo,* (Zhongguo) the Central Kingdom, seeing itself as a source of social ideals which had notable influence in neighboring kingdoms. These values are still recognized as important social elements in near by Asian countries, such as Korea and Japan, who consciously adopted the Confucian model as a means to establish political and social order until the modern era.

The role of China as a model for Asia changed drastically with the coming of European colonial expansion and economic exploitation during the 19th century. Whereas Japan was able to modernize, resist colonial aggression, and bring neighboring Korea, Okinawa, and the province of Taiwan under its rule, China's last Qing dynasty emperors (as common textbooks tell children) hid behind the protective walls of the Forbidden City and the Imperial lakeside villas while foreign nations carved off rich coastal cities, like slices of watermelon, for economic exploitation and political domination.

Children are taught in text books how French, German, American, and Russian exploitation were second only to the gross, immoral, even inhuman abuse imposed on China by England and Japan. The economic expansion of England from 1830 onwards depended in great part upon the Opium Trade with China. Great Britain, against the impotent resistance of poorly armed Qing dynasty troops, sold illegal substance (opium) along the south coast of China, using the silver bullion gained from this trade to build and support a colonial empire. Japan's rape of China from 1930 through 1945 still scars the memories of informants in chapter 3. Until today China has received no reparation or apology for Japanese wartime atrocities.

All of this changed with the establishing of the People's Republic in 1949. A formerly weak China, easily subjugated by western armies for more than 100 years, became a power to be feared and respected. The new China forced a stalemate with the United States in Korea in 1954, broke off close ties with Russia in 1956, went through collectivization (1955), a Great Leap into communization (1958), a Great Cultural Revolution (1966-78), and a total reversal of policy into capitalization and consumer profit from 1980 to the present.

As a result of these drastic changes, China is now rapidly becoming a wealthy nation, courted by the west for access to its rich markets. But the effects of economic growth, China's official press admits, have not all been positive. An abundance of food, new clothes, cars, television, washing machines, refrigerators, computers in many households, have brought a rise in crime of all sorts, the re-introduction of drugs, prostitution, and political corruption that were unknown during the halcyon years of Mao Tsedong's rule. In the words of a social science scholar:

> Today, after four decades of failure in the socialist revolu-
> tion, the government of China no longer serves as a model for
> conservative social values, Confucian, socialist, or Marxist. It
> has become, instead, a power broker of wealth and political
> favor. Privileged citizens and approved foreigners find immense
> profit in China's new economy, while the peasant farmers in
> the distant provinces still eke out a meager living. Workers laid
> off from failing state enterprises, and unemployed from the
> poorest provinces flock to the big cities, seeking employment
> and a better way of life for their families back home.

In the words of the same sociologist:

> Like cultural treasures of the past put on sale in antique
> markets, traditional family values are summoned forth like ske-
> letons from an old closet, to revive feelings of stability and
> and self-worth in a time when only quick profit matters in the
> life of public officials. The life of the ordinary people is not al-
> ways bettered in this process.... Family, in the minds of govern-
> ment officials and scholars, is the only stabilizing authority
> in modern China. (Unpublished paper, CASS, 1995).

The economic and psychological disasters of the Great Leap and the Cultural Revolution were mitigated, the stories of chapters 3 and 4 tell us, by the personal strength found in family support and obligation. That same strength is invoked today by those who are poor, jobless, or dependent on *Guanxi* personal relationships to make a living.

As another scholar at the same conference put it: "Today the only government decree taken seriously by the people of China is the slogan of Deng Xiaoping, *To get rich is glorious.*"

In adopting the cliché "Socialism with a peculiar Chinese flavor," government leaders admit publicly that the best defense against social lawlessness, political corruption, and public outrage is the revival of traditional values from China's suppressed past. Of these concepts, family life, devoted friendship, and political loyalty, are proclaimed to be most crucial. (ibid.)

2) The Scholar'sView of the Chinese Family

It is important for our study to explain, as well, what the traditional scholar from the past took to be essential Chinese family virtues. The Confucian system, described in the *Analects (Lun-yü)* attributed to Confucius, makes the virtue of *hsiao (xiao)*, translated sometimes as filiality, but referring more precisely to the virtues engendered by parent-child relationships, as the basic virtue of human life. *Yi* reciprocal obligation, treats friends like brothers and sisters. *Jen* (pronounced "ren") welcomes all men and women with the benevolence of a family member. *Li*, which means respect, is, in the etymological derivation of the Chinese pictograph, an offering of food and song for spirits during ritual, and the offering of sustenance (food, drink and song, poetry, conversation) and respect when a guest comes into the home.

These values make the nation into a family (the word for nation in Chinese is *kuo-chia, i.e.,* a family kingdom). "Within the four seas, all men are brothers," sang Confucius of the Chinese cultural system. The good king must be endowed with these family oriented virtues, to be mandated by heaven (*tianming*) to rule.

The teachings of the great Taoist sage Lao-tzu, contained in the *Tao-te Ching (Daode Jing)* are just as explicit about the basic fatherly and motherly qualities of the Tao in gestating nature. The Tao gives birth to the One, i.e., cosmic mother, *Ch'i (Qi)* primordial breath, continually hovering and breathing ("*inspiratio*") life into the cosmos. The One gives birth to the Two, primordial spirit, yang, the male aspects of the cosmos; then rests and gives birth to the Three, primordial essence, the yin, female aspects of nature. Tao and Nature are father and mother; all humanity and nature are Tao's children.

The Confucian system is to the social family as is the Taoist world view to the human family vis-a-vis nature. Man and woman, in this Taoist sense, are equal, with woman (water, yin) given a superior role in the sense of nourishing, gestating, and closeness to Tao.

The great heroes of the Confucian and Taoist systems, re-mythologized during the Han dynasty (200 BCE to 200 ACE), share a common folk origin. Besides the Three Ancient Rulers Yao, Shun, and Yü, whom both systems recognized for their family centered virtues, a second set of five legendary emperors, the *Wu-ti* of the Yin-yang Five Element cosmology, were re-invented, to place further importance and value on the family as a function of cosmic order. With them was created a pantheon of spiritual rulers, honored in the village temples and household altars throughout China. These mythological heroes form the basis for village and family festival and worship, providing models for family and village community life.

The ancient Yin-yang Five Element cosmology was adapted by scholars of the late Warring States period (5th to 3rd centuries B.C.), to establish order in a period of political chaos. Modern villages and families of China still offer rites of "*dulia*" respect to the Five Ancient Emperors and a panoply of folk heroes, who founded and continue to nourish all aspects of Chinese family life.

Fu Hsi, mythical emperor of the East, founded the Chinese family. With his wife Nü Kua he rules over spring, presides over the greening of nature, and blesses marriage and the home in China. Shen Nung, Red Emperor of the south, is patron of agriculture and the nourishment of the family. Huang-ti, Yellow Emperor of the center, and his wife invented sericulture (the weaving of silk into clothes), medicine for healing, and the *Kuo-chia (Guojia)* nation-family political system. Shao-hao, white-robed ruler of the west, and Chuan-hsü purple-robed king of the north, govern burial and ancestor ritual. The complete cycle of the family rites of passage are held together by the

6

watchful protection of ancestors and spirits from the after life. The cosmology of ancient China, the annual calendar of festivals, and the household ancestor shrine affirm the importance of family life.

Traditional rites of passage, i.e., birth, puberty, marriage, burial, and ancestor respect, existed before the crafting of the intellectually justifying Yin-yang Five Element system. The later cosmology was made to fit a pristine social system, in the earliest of Chinese literary works, the ancient *Book of Odes*, and the *I-ching* (*Book of Changes*).

Almost a fourth of the *Book of Odes*, (translated with depth of feeling by Arthur Waley, and in more sober terms by James Legge and Bernhard Karlgren), sing of the rites of courtship and lovemaking in early China. In a celebrated passage, a zither-strumming maiden begs her loved one Chung-tzu to seek parental permission before entering the family precincts.

Chung-tzu, do not come through the mulberry trees (village);
I love you dearly, but I fear what my parents will say.
Chung-tzu, do not come through the cassia trees (family compound), It's not that I don't love you, but I fear what brothers (friends) will say.
Chung-tzu, don't come through the willows (into my home)
I love you dearly, but I fear what the villagers will say.

The meeting of a lover, courtship, and marriage were themes that shocked many later scholars who wondered why the sage Confucius included such worldly verses in a work otherwise dedicated to court rites and festivals.

The traditional scholar answers, in a gloss to the text, that proper courtship and marriage precede the forming of family, and therefore have an important role in the social-ritual system.

For the ordinary people of China, therefore, the family is the center and focus of village and household life. Festivals, rites of passage, economic success, health care, and psychological support are all a part of its function The spirits of the past and the powers of the present work to preserve this nourishing system.

The importance Confucius placed on the forming of family relationships are also found in the most ancient of all Chinese writings, the *Book of Changes*. This cryptic text, included in Confucian and Taoist classics, is composed of a series of eight hexagrams, i.e., six broken and unbroken lines representing change in nature, and a series of sixty-four statements concerning the meaning of these changes.

The *I-ching's* eight trigrams are named after the ideal Chinese family, that is, father, mother, older, middle, and younger brother, older, middle, and younger sister. The combination of eight-times-eight trigrams make up the sixty-four hexagrams, exhausting the total number of changes possible in a hexadecimal system.

The genius of the Chinese mind is seen in the symbolic expression of this binary system in terms of the cosmic Chinese family. The three unbroken lines that represent the yang or male force of nature are called "father," while the six broken lines that represent the female gestatrix are called "mother" of all nature. The very cosmic structure of reality as expressed in the eight trigrams is synonymous with the idealized notion of the family.

One of the most important works attributed to Confucius is the *Book of Rites*, which since the Han Dynasty (200 BC to 200 AD), governed the family rites of passage, i.e., birthing, puberty, marriage, burial and ancestor ritual. One of the duties of the state-appointed mandarins who were assigned to office in the provinces, after passing the three levels of civil service exams based on the Confucian classics, was to regulate and report on local variations of the authorized form of the family rites of passage.

The *Beijing Gazetteer 1812-1912*, one hundred years of Imperial Court proceedings, which were gathered by the British Consul in Beijing, and stored in the State Paper Room of the British Museum, bear eloquent testimony to the zeal of the mandarins in reporting on the correct observance of marriage and burial ritual. Besides overseeing the collecting of taxes, the Yamen public offices of the provincial and Hsien-district administration filled page after page of briefs on the ritual and festive practice in the areas where they resided.

From these and many other texts that emphasize the importance of ritual and festival centered on family, we can judge the emphasis that the Chinese state placed on maintaining the integrity of familial life in China. Every detail of ritual and festival surrounding the family rites of passage were prescribed by national law. This concern for ritual at the national level was offset by variation and adaptation at the village and family level, prompting the Han dynasty redactor of the *Book of Rites* to quote the proverb:

> When entering the nation, listen to the laws.
> Entering the village, inquire about customs.
> Entering the family, learn the taboos.

The central role of family life in China even in the present day is confirmed by the life stories and experiences recounted in chapters 2, 3, and 4. Though the manner of building the family through various forms of marriage and customs may be different for Taiwan, North China, and the minority cultures of the west and southwest, the family continues to function as a source of stability, in a nation beleaguered by change and unrest.

3) *Foreign Views of the Chinese Family*

The works of foreign scholars on the Chinese family, or Chinese scholars trained abroad such as Fei Xiaotong, give a much more pessimistic, even negative view of the traditional family, when compared with the idealistic descriptions of the classics. Arthur Wolf and Huang Chieh-shan's *Marriage and Adoption in China*, Margery Wolf's *The House of Lim*, and many of the families described in chapters 2, 3 and 4 show a China filled with human sorrow and tragedy, as well as with the joys of courtship, building a family, bearing children, and enjoying the festive life of a Chinese household.

Whatever conclusions are to be drawn from studies that emphasize the negative or focus on the positive, the basic rule stated in our premise remains the same; the family constitutes the basic social unit required for survival in China. From the immense variety of marriage forms described in the work of Arthur Wolf and many others, we can surmise that any and all means must be taken to build a family, surrogate or real, in order to survive in traditional and modern China.

When entering the villages, districts, and provinces of China, an immense variety of customs and local practices overwhelm the research scholar. Some foreign observers believe that there are no constant norms for marriage, family values, or household customs in

China. Chinese scholars, on the other hand, argue for a structural homogeneity of ritual practice. Arthur Wolf's *Religion and Ritual in China* provides a number of scholarly articles on the topic. The preface of Arthur Wolf, and the last essay of Robert Smith, recapitulate a stimulating dialogue with the late Maurice Freedman. A. Wolf and R. Smith emphasize unique local differences, while Maurice Freedman, in the tradition of the British social anthropologist looks for dominant and universal patterns and roles.

4) *Our Choice of Methodology and Sources for Studying the Family*

Due to the use of similar household registers, the methodology of Arthur Wolf and Huang Chieh-shan became the basis for the statistical portion of our study. We found, however, that due to immense differences in farm and city households. the Haishan statistics were a sharp contrast to the Hsinchu data. The Wolf-Huang formulation of a methodology for studying the family were, nevertheless, an inspiration and guide for our own study.

We can ask why the Haishan district was so different from other parts of China. One of the causes may have been the proximity with the red light district of Banka in Taipei city. The fact that 70 percent of all girls in Haishan were adopted out by age ten as *simpua* child bride-to-be, the number of *hsiao-nü*, i.e., "filial" adopted daughters sold into the prostitution trade, and many other economic and social factors make Haishan-Shulin a special case. The high number of child bride-to-be adoptions seems peculiar to the Hai-shan Shulin area, perhaps due to the fact that so many were sold into the night-life trade in the nearby Banka district of Taipei.

The Hsinchu families are closer to the statistical data supplied by Okada Jun of the nearby Shih-lin area in the Taipei basin, the study of Sophie Sa of the Ku-ting area of Taipei city, and the legal works of Suzuki and Aneba quoted extensively in chapter 5. (See Okada, Jun, *Kiso Shakai* (*The Basic Structure of Chinese Society*), Taipei, 1947; Sa, Sophie, *The Chinese Family of the Ku-ting Area in Taipei*, unpublished doctoral dissertation, 400 pp.).

We believe that certain aspects of the family found in the Hsinchu statistics show what traditional Chinese scholars consider to be

10

ideal. Other elements point to a more basic need, the building of the family by any means necessary. The variations found in the registers suggest that without family of some form or other, life is not livable in China.

We are deeply indebted, in our research, to the publications of Niida Noboru, who established the origin of the *simpua* child-bride practice in his T'ang and Sung dynasty studies, and to the statistical reports on the Chinese family issued by the Academy of Social Sciences in Beijing. This latter study gives details of marriages, fertility, divorce, and other aspects of modern Chinese family life, demonstrating great structural changes in the Chinese family due to the one child rule, which statistics show is observed for the most part in the city, by couples with a higher education. Farming families (and party cadres) we note, tend to build larger families.

The views of the common people, the overwhelming size of the Chinese population, the desperate need for food, space, and the necessities of a human life, which surpass the powers of the imagination to analyze without first-hand observation, are treated in the last chapter of our work. The prosperity of China in the future, the limitation of family size, the bettering of the way of life for the masses by the increase of production, the rebuilding of cultural festivals and rituals in the socialist state, are goals sought by the families of modern China. The education of children, the building of a prosperous family, the enjoyment of life centered on the family hearth and familial relationships, continue to motivate and bring vitality to the Chinese social system, no matter what political or social changes occur outside its protective boundaries.

NARRATIVES OF CHINESE FAMILY LIFE

2. CASE STUDIES OF CHINESE FAMILIES IN TAIWAN

From the 4,500 families (20,000 individuals) analyzed in the statistical section of our study, we have randomly chosen five case histories to present here in a more personal perspective. By so doing, we hope to shed some light on why certain choices were made, such as preferring a *simpua* child bride over a *yangnü* servant girl for adoption. Since the circumstances found in the household registers are confidential in nature, the identity of the household and the individuals who reside within its "doorway" have therefore been carefully encoded, so as to preserve privacy for the living family and its relatives.

The personal stories from the household registers tell of adoptions, uxorilocal marriages, division of households, and death in a far more eloquent way than can be imagined from statistics. We see that, in fact, the various forms of marriage, adoption, and even the bringing of a lodger into the household can be directly or indirectly related to enhancing family life, for health care or economic well being. The tendency to increase the number of people residing in the household cannot be accounted for simply by assigning a Confucian or other generic value to a frequently observed phenomenon. The details presented in chapter 2 depict very human and emotional reasons for changes in family composition, both deliberate, such as adoption, marriage, divorce, division, and bringing in a lodger, and forces outside family control, such as death, infertility, and failure in business.

It would be scientifically impossible to assign a generic cause for the choices open to a family for marriage (major, minor, uxorilocal, concubine) or adoption (*kuo-fang-tzu* related, or *ming-ling-tzu* unrelated boy; *simpua, yangnü,* or *cabogan* slave girl) occur in the family registers of chapter 6. Yet by examining the anecdotes that families tell about these changes, we can perhaps discover some very human reasons for the choices made behind the household door that provided the social scientist's cold count. The view from the warmth of the family hearth gives a different perspective to life within the Chinese household.

Our plan in chapter 2 is to present a brief history of each family in summary form, derived from the kinship charts used in the statistical counts of chapter 6. The reader unfamiliar with kinship terms can easily grasp the information provided herein by referring to the following abbreviations, which are useful to remember:

a = grandson HH =household head

a¹ = granddaughter HHH =heir to household head

AI = adopted in K = *kuo-fang-tzu*, adopted boy

AL = absentee landlord   with the same surname

AO = adopted out ML =*ming-ling tzu*; any other

DM =date of marriage   boy adoption

B = birthdate M = major marriage

C = concubine m =minor marriage

CC = concubine's child 1,2,3 =1,2,3 son or daughter

CH = uxorilocal husband 01 = father of HH, grandfather

    (*chao-hsü*) 02 = mother of HH

CM = concubine marriage PM = Peimen, Northgate area;

DA = dissolved adoption   (whence the data is taken).

DC = district change   Other districts are:

DH = divided household HS = Hsimen (Westgate), and the

DE = dissolved engagement   many farming districts to

DV = divorce   the NW and W of the city

    of Hsinchu. The South and

DM = date of marriage   East areas are omitted

E = employee S = *simpua*, girl

Fa = father   child brought in to be a

Gr = grandfather   bride for a son.

F 1,2,3, = daughter 1,2,3 Y= *Yangnü*, girl child adopted

FHH = female house-head   to be a quasi-servant

GSS = general supply store Z = girl purchased as a slave

(N.B. The above abbreviations are special to this study; they do not represent standard sociological usage in constructing kinship charts for other studies. Dates are listed by year/day/ month).

Case 1. Bamboo Craftsman   (Code: PS 12-8)

1889 Beginning of the household register. The wife of the future heir to the household head (HH) is registered into the family on 1/2, when her first son is born, 23/10.

1891 The father of the HH dies, and the husband is made the new

16

household head. He formally married the mother of his son, and registered the marriage as occuring on 26/11.

1896   A second son is born on 9/8.

1920   The eldest son marries a sixteen year old girl on 5/12.

1921   The sixteen year old divorces her husband and moves out 29/4.

1922   The second son of the HH dies on 15/7.

1923   The first son takes an eighteen year old second wife, 22/7.

1924   A daughter is born to the second wife, 23/1, six months later.

1925   The second wife divorces her husband, moves out, 1/1.

1937   The HH dies at age 68, and is succeeded by his son.

The household register ends, when the HH moves away.

***

The family of the randomly chosen bamboo craftsman is certainly not typical of the traditional Confucian model. All of the children born over a forty-eight year period were conceived out of wedlock, or, before the marriage was officially registered. Two divorces occur during the household registration. As if the place had something to do with the continuing misfortune, the family moves away after the death of the household head. Neighbors, however, remembered the family and its problems.

Examining the families adjacent to this household, we find that other neighbors were also famous for inconstancy in marriage. The most famous neighbor was a herpetologist, with a total of three wives, three concubines, and twenty-two children over a forty-seven year period. The grandfather, the present generation relates, threatened to kill himself by letting a cobra bite him, each time he wanted to rid himself of a wife. The first two wives were convinced by grandfather's threats, and dutifully left the family after the *liyuan* divorce papers were filed with the Japanese authorities. But the third wife refused to go. It seems she had figured out grandfather's ploy, or so her grandchildren relate. Grandfather first milked the fangs of the cobra, then let it bite him. Third grandmother refused to move, and waited for grandfather to recover. Her son inherited the business, and runs the shop today.

The bamboo craftsman and other families moved away because of the "tea house" that operated on the corner, which provided a flourishing night life business. Divorces occurred when new wives were taken from madames who operated out of the tea house. Economic prosperity and the building of a high rise apartment brought an end to the night life trade. The tea house moved away, but the herpetologist still maintains a thriving business, and a flourishing one wife family.

Case 2. A Coolie family, with a female HH after 1917

The second case study shows how a *yang-nü* girl can be adopted into a family to be the heir to the appointed household head, when the birth of children to other members of the extended family challenge the household head's authority.

1901   The household registration begins with the birth of a second son to the retired household head, on 5/3. The child is a younger brother of the young HH2, and uncle to the future female household head (FHH).

1903   Birth of a second daughter to the retired HH1, 5/6. Death of the first wife of the former HH1 occurs after the second daughter's birth.

1907   The young HH2 marries an eighteen year old girl on 13/12.

1910   A forty-two year old female marries the father, HH1. Note that this is grandfather's second marriage.

1912   A twelve year old girl is adopted in as a *yang-nü* (Y) of the childless young HH2, on 14/1. This child becomes the FHH on the death of her adoptive father in 1917. Birth of a male, illegitimate son of an older sister of the now sickly HH2.

1917   Death of HH2. The *yang-nü* is made new FHH. Death of the father, HH1.

1919   9/5, death of the second wife of HH1. 25/5 a fifteen year old girl marries the brother of HH1. 1/11, sister of the former HH moves out, in order to marry (marriage cannot take place for three years in a family where a death has occurred). Her illegitimate son stays behind. 20/11, wife of HH2 moves out.

1921   A son is born to the brother of HH1, on 3/10.

1923   A daughter is born to the brother of HH1 on 30/11, but dies shortly after on 21/12.

1925   A second son is born to the brother of HH1, 19/6.

1927 A second daughter is born to the brother of HH1, 13/8.

1929 The second daughter is adopted out, 26/11, as a *simpua*.

1935 The first wife of the brother divorces, and moves out, on 27/10. Within two weeks the brother marries a second wife on 8/11.

1937 The brother (uncle of FHH) decides to take his share of the household (divided household, DH) and move out. The illegitimate son follows his uncle, and is registered into the uncle's new household. The FHH sells house and moves out. The register is closed.

***

The adoption of a *yang-nü* daughter rather than a *simpua* in the above case insured the eldest son's (adopted) child the position of heir to the household headship. This girl, sold by her parents to be an adopted daughter of the young, childless household head in 1912, provided health care for the aging grandfather (HH1) and for her adoptive father (HH2), who was too weak to pull the heavy carts and earn enough money to support the growing coolie family. As his health worsened, the teenage girl was called upon to cook for the entire family, manage accounts, and nurse her ailing "father" and grandfather.

When her "father" died in 1917, the family agreed that this kindly and patient girl be made a female HH, to alleviate the continuing disputes between the younger brother, his wife, and sister who meanwhile had given birth to an illegitimate child. Since custom prohibited marriage within three years of the HH's death, the sister moved out of the house to marry, leaving behind her illegitimate son to continue working in the coolie family. Finally the brother and his second wife demand that the house be sold, to get their share of the inheritance and establish their own household. Left alone, the (now) thirty-seven year old FHH officially closes the register, and moves in with a neighbor widower's family.

Though the household register does not record the trauma and distress that occasioned the various choices made by the coolie family, it is clear from the bare details of the registry office that the life of the second brother was plagued by divorce, disputes, and strife. Once the family was dissolved, however, the fortunes of the former FHH improved immensely. Her new husband, a widower with one son, a coolie who pulled heavy loads on a two-wheel cart, plied his trade from a shack on a street corner of the busy Northgate district. With the small amount of money coming to her from the sale of the estate, she was able to purchase a one-room residence for her new family to live in.

When her adoptive son came of age, he married the daughter of the blacksmith, who lived next door. Between them, the young coolie and his wife had six children, the last two of which were twin boys. Again providing care and affection, the former FHH, now a grandmother, cooked, took care of her new family, and led a quiet life, seeing her grandchildren through high school and college. Two of the grandchildren opened a woodwork shop, exporting wood carvings and hand made furniture to overseas businesses. Today the family lives in a three story mansion, with grateful memories of the (now) deceased grandmother who brought stability and affluence to a coolie family.

Case 3. A Farmer's Family   (PS 14-41)

In the third example, the household head was born on 9/5/1886. He became HH1 on 15/5/1901, when 21.9 years old. His wife was born 2/7/1887, and was a widow with a son from a first marriage when she married and was registered into her second husband's home on 2/5/1908. The stories of a *simpua* child bride and her *chao-hsü* uxorilocal husband are told in the narrative accompanying this case study.

1908   The wife of HH1 is registered into the household, 5/2.

1911   The couple adopt Y1, a *yang-nü* girl 1.1 years old, 25/9.

1925   The son of the wife by her first marriage is called into the household to be a *chao-hsü* uxorilocal husband for the adopted girl, 20/9. She is 15.1 yrs old; he (uxorilocal husband) is 21.9.

1926   HH1 and his wife adopt Y2, a second *yang-nü* girl, age 9.10, on 20/1. The first *yang-nü* (Y1) gives birth to a daughter, who is given the HH's family surname (adoptive mother's name).

1929   A first son is born to the *yang-nü; he* is also given the HH1's family name, on 1/9. Y2, second *yang-nü* is adopted out to Lang-kang, a farming area, the same day.

1932   A second son is born to the *yang-nü* (Y1) on 13/5. This son is given the uxorilocal father's name (P= paternal name).

1935   A third son is born to Y1 and the Uxorilocal husband on 10/12;

the boy, given the father's surname, dies four days later, 4/12.

1938 A fourth son, born on 18/3, is given the father's name.

1939 HH1 dies, 23/1. The eldest son of Y1 and the uxorilocal husband, who was given the deceased HH1's surname, becomes the new HH2.

***

We can see how in the above case the adoption of a *yang-nü* rather than a *simpua* was essential to maintain the family line of the childless farmer (PS 41-14). A *simpua* girl must legally keep her own surname, and thus when married to an uxorilocal husband, her children could not be given the family name. The childless couple (the husband was presumably infertile, since the wife had a son by a previous liaison) needed an heir to receive the farmer's land and continue the family line. The couple had the choice of adopting a son from a family with the same surname (*kuo-fang-tzu*), or a different surname (*ming-ling-tzu*), or else adopting a girl who took the surname of the adopting family, and bore children by an uxorilocal husband.

For this farming family the choice of an adopted girl and an uxorilocal husband, which we see from the statistics of chapters 6 and 7 was favored in low income families, proved the most convenient. Just in case the first adopted girl was not fertile, a second girl (Y2) was adopted. But after the first child's birth ten months later, the Y2 was adopted out. Since the family now had an heir, and further uxorilocal husbands were unnecessary, it was no longer practical to raise a second *yang-nü*. The oldest son of the couple, who was given the deceased HH1's surname, becomes the new HH2 at age 9.5. The uxorilocal husband (father of the new HH2) was 35.2, and the *yang-nü* mother 28.7 when their son was made household head. Niida, Okuda, and Suzuki remind us, however, (see ch. 5, note 1) that the young HH was bound to obey his mother and father until mature, by customary law.

Case 4. *An Absentee Landlord* (PS 12-15)

The next case is far more complicated than the fairly simple and straightforward worker, coolie, and farmer. The absentee landlord, who on mainland China bore the brunt of the wrath of Mao Tse-tung and the People's Republic after 1949, became the basis of Taiwan's land reform and later industrial development, through landlords' and international investments on Taiwan. The wealthy families of the late Ch'ing dynasty gentry, whose names appear in the local gazetteers and histories, maintained political and economic dominance throughout the Japanese colonial occupation well into the modern period. To maintain the family line and family business, and to invest family funds after land reform in such a way that the family fortunes prospered, became the key to success for the entrepreneurial landlords of Hsinchu and the other cities of Taiwan.

The present case study follows the fortunes of a wealthy North-gate (Peimen) family from the late Ch'ing period up to the beginning of the second World War, 1883-1937. The register shows that all possible means were used to maintain the wealth and strength of the family line, by *kuo-fang-tzu* adoptions, i.e., by adopting sons of the same surname, from within the family clan line. The family is thus assured continuity over a period of unpredictable and sometimes violent change.

1883 Beginning of the household with marriage of the absentee landlord (HH1) and his wife, on 6/4.

1884 A first son is born, in the eighth month.

1893 An affinal relative is registered as a slave girl, 2/2 (Z1). (The register is falsified; Z1 is a consanguinal relative).

1894 A second relative registered as a slave, 3/5 (Z2).

1903 A slave registered in to the wife's quarters, 10-/1 (Z3).

1904 An eighteen year old girl marries the eldest son, and brings with her a slave girl (Z4), on 16/6.

1907 The two relatives (Z1 and Z2) change their status to that of *simpua*, girls brought in as future brides, (S1, S2).

1908 The eldest son and his wife, who are childless, adopt in a son from a branch clan, as a *kuo-fang-tzu*, (related on the father's side, same surname), on 17/5 (K1). The wife brings in her own slave girl (Z5) on 25/8.

1909 The eldest *simpua* S1 adopts in her own young *simpua*(S3). S1 and S2 become the owners of an expensive courtesan club catering to Japanese officials.

1910 S2 adopts in her own *simpua* (S4), 3/8, to work in the night club. Wife of the eldest son buys a second slave girl (Z6), 25/3.

1914   The eldest son and wife adopt in a second *kuo-fang-tzu* son (K2), on 25/5. S2 adopts a *yang-nü* daughter on 16/6 (Y1), to create her own household.

1915   S1 adopts in two *yang-nü* girls, Y2 and Y3, while S4 adopts her very own *yang-nü* daughter, on 28/5 (Y5).

1916   S2 adopts a second *yang-nü* (Y6) on 29/10.

1917   The wife of the eldest son buys a third slave girl, Z6, who is registered into the family on 15/6.

1918   The first son admits that he has two concubines, C1 and C2, who are formally registered in to the household on 22/3. The second concubine C2 gives birth to a daughter soon after, 10/4.

1919   HH1 head changes the status of Z3 to that of a concubine on 30/5. The first son follows suit, and changes the status of Z4 to that of his concubine on 16/5. HH1 "retires" on 20/5, making his eldest son heir to the household (HH2). C3, concubine of retired HH1, is pregnant, and is made to move out of the home   by the first wife.

1920   C3 gives birth to a daughter, and allows the infant to be registered in retired HH1's household on 15/8, when the child is ten months old. The *simpua* S3 of the eldest aunt dies on 23/11.

1921   The new household head (HH2) and his wife send back their second adopted son (K2) to his original parents on 15/5. The eldest aunt S1 adopts another daughter on the same day, Y6.

1922-3 HH2 and his wife adopt out the girl born to C2, second concubine on 1/2. They also adopt out the girl born to C3, the retired HH1's concubine ten months later, on 1/12. HH1 dies shortly later, the first month of 1923.

1925-6 S1 adopts in her fourth *yang-nü* girl, Y7, on 2/1. HH2 dissolves the relationship between C2's daughter (DA) and the household, on 9/6. HH2 brings in a fourth concubine (C5) on 1/11, who gives birth to a daughter on 6/11. On 26/4/1926 S1 dissolves the adoption of Y7, and sends her back to her family.

1927   Z6, the slave girl of the HH's wife, moves out, 8/5. S2's adopted daughters Y1 and Y6 each adopt daughter for themselves (Y8, Y9) on 1/6. All of the adopted daughters of the elder aunts are changed to the status of lodgers in the household, 12/7, due to differences with HH2's wife.

1928   C2 (second concubine of the HH2) gives birth to a girl, 9/1. S3 (*simpua* of S1) aunt adopts in her own girl, Y10, on 1/3. Note that the two elder aunts now have their own independent household of twelve women, and live as lodgers with HH2, outside the influence of HH2's wife.

1930   The adopted son of the HH2, (K1) marries a seventeen year-old girl on 10/4. On the same day they adopt two girls as *yang-nü*, Y11 and Y12. The adopted girls are eleven and seven years old, respectively.

1931   C2, (HH2's second concubine) gives birth to a son on 1/3. HH2's wife refuses to admit this child into the family; he is adopted out on 11/6. HH2 takes a fifth concubine (C6) on 31/12. Meanwhile, Y3 (S2's second adopted daughter) adopts in her own daughter, Y13, on 30/5. Y2 (S1's first adopted daughter) also adopts Y14, on 2/6. Y10 (Y2's adopted daughter) adopts a girl (Y16) on 24/6, bringing the family of lady lodgers to fifteen, and making elder auntie S1 into a great-grandmother by adoption.

1932-3 The fortunes of the family begin to wane, as the health of HH2 deteriorates. Members of the household begin to move out. A son is born to K1, HH2's adopted son, 16/1/1932, but the child dies 16/2/1933. Y12, his second adopted daughter, is sold out to another family on 20/12/1933. The daughter of the deceased HH1's concubine C3 leaves, 15/6. Y10 then gives her adopted daughter to Y6 (her sister) on 23/12 and moves out on 24/12. C5, the fourth concubine of the HH2, gives birth to two girls, on 3/3/1932, and 3/3/1933.

1934   A first son is born to HH2 and C5, his fourth concubine, 16/4. The status of Z5 and Z7, his two slave girls, is changed to lodgers, on 5/6, as the health of HH2 further deteriorates.

1935   The Japanese colonial government imposes a district change in the numbering of households in Northgate.

24

1936 The son of C2, the third concubine, who was adopted out is again brought into the family, 6/2; his former adoption is dissolved. A second son is born to C5, HH2's fourth concubine, 20/4. A girl is born to the HH2's eldest son, K1. This birth makes it possible for the eldest son K1 to be heir to the HH.

1937 Y2, the second adopted daughter of eldest aunt, adopts her own *yang-nü* girl (Y16) on 31/3. The HH dies. His adopted son K1 is heir to the household.

***

The Japanese registration office was hard put to keep accurate account of such complicated family relations. When the household registers (*koseki*) were initiated in 1906, the head of each household was asked to recall the history of the family, as best he or she could. In the above case, the elder household head recorded his wife's sisters as slave girls (mand: *ya-t'ou*; pronounce *za-bo-gan* in Taiwanese). The status was later changed to that of *simpua* or girls brought into the family to be brides of a son. In fact the term is seen to be cosmetic, hiding any number of complex family relationships from the uncomprehending and hopelessly bureaucratic Japanese authorities. The two aunties were in fact residents in their brother-in-law's wealthy household, and lived for the most part outside the control of the household heads and their wives.

In fact, the "adopted" girls, sisters of the wife of the household head, were both extremely successful courtesans in Hsinchu's best night club, that catered to Japanese officials. Both were lesbian, detesting men and refusing to marry, whether as a result of their night life trade, preference, or other reasons. The adoption of daughters and *ming-ling-tzu* sons was therefore a viable way to build their own families. Over a thirty year period, they became first surrogate mothers, then grandmothers. The affairs of the two families, wealthy landlord and lesbian courtesans, did not impinge on each other. Of the two, the unwed grandmothers provided a far more stable home environment than the wealthy landlord and his competing concubines.

The two ladies were able to build their own independent household by adoption. The girls adopted by the two unwed sisters were classified first as *simpua*, then as *yang-nü*, but in fact none of them married from the beginning of the household registration until the establishing of the new register in 1937.

This kind of an example, i.e., a household composed entirely of female members is seen repeatedly in the Hsinchu family registers. Women who worked as courtesans, prostitutes, or other night life related professions, could not marry in the city where they worked, except as concubines. They could dwell as lodgers in their original family residence, or live separately with one female chosen to be the household head.

Chinese custom strictly forbade first marriages of the upper class landlords, merchants, or gentry with women of the night life professions. The two aunts from the upper gentry class chose to adopt daughters, to build a family of their own. That the women functioned as a logical family unit is clear from the register. Daughters were adopted at regular intervals, presumably to work in the family business, as well as to maintain the household for the older working members. The household head eventually registered the adopted girls as "lodgers," a move taken to satisfy the registration office as well as the demands of *shen-fen*, i.e., the "customary" (szu-fa) law of social status.

HH1, the elder household head, on the other hand, and his only son who was HH2 between 1917 and 1937, were allowed not only to have concubines and other liaisons, but obviously used their slave girls in a quasi-concubine relationship. The son not only declared his first slave girl a concubine, but developed four other concubine relationships before his death in 1937 at age fifty-three.

Even though his fourth concubine bore him two sons, the strength of the matriarch of the family, his first wife, was such that her favorite adopted son K1 became family head in 1937. Though unable to bear children herself, the first son's wife seems to have dominated the household from within, as soon as her husband was made HH2 in 1917. Her role is subordinated to her adopted son and his wife when the family begins a new registration in 1937.

As will be seen in chapter 5, more than 12% of the Hsinchu families had female household heads (FHH), whether as registered uxorilocal matriarchs, unmarried single women, or widows. Such a phenomenon was much less likely to occur in the much more conservaive farming villages of Shulin and Haishan in the Taipei basin to the north of Hsinchu.

Case Five. A Fabric Dyer   (PS 20-28)

The case of the fabric dyer is the most complex, and at the same time the most straightforward of our five family histories. The family history can be traced from 1887 until 1946, the beginning of the modern registration system, and thenceforth into the present. Our study carries us from the family's inception in 1887 up to the beginning of the modern period in 1946. We can follow the development of the household from a simple nuclear form, through the extended, and grand family structure. Since both male and female members of the family were required to work in the business of fabric dying, the household maintains the extended and grand structural forms through most of its history.

This case history is particularly useful because we can find within the fifty years or so covered by the kinship chart almost every form of adoption and marriage pattern. *Yang-nü* and *simpua* girl adoptions, *chao-hsü* uxorilocal marriages, and the assigning of the children born from the marriage to the mother and father's lineage, are seen in this register. Some of the sons chose new professions and moved out. Others remained a part of the family business, functioning as multiple households under one roof. The family fortunes are intimately wrapped up in the very structure of the family itself.

1887   28/3, birth of the eldest son (to become the second household head HH2) to HH1 and his *simpua* wife (mother age 19).

1889   10/7 birth of second son (YB1, mother age 21.7).

1900   26/5 birth of third son (YB2, mother age 32.4).

1906   16/10 birth of fourth son (YB3 mother age 38.7). 10/11 marriage of eldest son, HH2, who is 19.7 with a 18.11- year old girl, (W of HH2).

1907   27/10 birth of the first daughter (F1) to HH2 and his wife.

1909   12/6 marriage of YB1 with a twenty year old wife YB1W.

1912   21/1 birth of a first son to YB1 and wife.

1917   ?/11 adoption of a 3.2-year-old *ming-ling-tzu* boy by HH2, to insure an heir to the household head. Note that this boy eventually becomes the HH in 1945, after he has as son in 1944.

1918 18/1 marriage of younger brother YB2 to a 15.6-year-old girl.

1919 29/10 birth of a first daughter to YB2 and wife (16.4 yrs).

1924 11/3 birth of twin girls to YB2 and wife. One of the twins, not registered into the household, is adopted out at birth.

1925 23/10 marriage of third younger brother YB3 to a 19.8-year-old girl. (N.B., he is 19.0).

1926 3/5 death of HH1, age not specified, (40+). HH2 becomes the new household head. 30/6 birth of third daughter (4th child) to YB2 and wife. 20/8 birth of a first daughter to YB3 and wife. 18/12 YB2, as yet without male offspring, adopts a *ming-ling-tzu* boy who is four months old.

1927 2/1 death of YB2's 3rd daughter (4th child). 20/2 death of YB3, the third brother of HH. His wife is left a widow at 20.4, child 6 months old.

1928 25/3 F1, eldest daughter of HH1, takes an uxorilocal husband. She is 20.4, he is 21.7. Her younger adopted *ming-ling-tzu* brother (becomes HH in 1946) is 13.6. 14/6 A fifth daughter is born to YB2. 5/7 The eldest daughter F1 and her uxorilocal husband adopt a *yang-nü* daughter from nearby PS 20-44, a maker of rice cakes. The *yang-nü* is given uxorilocal husband's surname. 1/9 YB2 agrees to adopt out his fifth daughter (age 2 mo.). 3/9 YB2 adopts in Y1, a *yang-nü* girl, age 6.3, from nearby PS11-8,

1929 22/9 YB2's fifth daughter moves to her adoptive home, the village of Chin-kang, when 1.2 years old.

1930 1/2 YB2 (second younger brother) adopts a *yang-nü* girl as a second adopted daughter, from Shui-t'ien street #214. (Note that YB2 and family move to Shui-t'ien St. #216 in 1932). 22/11 YB1's eldest son marries; groom is 18.10, bride is 17.3 years old.

1931 31/11 The wife of the HH2 dies, age 43.11. HH2 is 44.7 at the time of his wife's death.

1932 18/3 The HH marries a second wife from Southgate (Nanmen) district inside the city, four months after his first wife's death. On the same day he recognizes her son, age 1.9 as his own eldest son, and adopts in a *simpua* (age 9.6) child bride who comes with the second wife. 13/4 All three of the younger brothers divide the family fortune, and move out to Shui-t'ien St. #216, where they establish an independent household. 6/7 F1 (eldest daughter of HH2) and her uxorilocal husband give birth to a son, who takes the mother's (HH2's) name. 7/9 A sister of the HH2, not yet entered into the household register, who had been adopted out as a *simpua* at her birth in 1902 before the register was begun, divorces her husband and moves in with the HH2 and her aging mother.

1933   10/4 The newly recognized sister moves to P'u-ting district, into her own new household (FHH).

1934   21/1 F1, the eldest daughter of HH and her uxorilocal husband give birth to a first daughter, and move to a branch store in T'ai-chung city (central Taiwan). 24/5 The HH's second wife gives birth to a second son. 8/7 The HH's adopted son (19.7) marries a 17.9-year-old girl from a nearby household in the Northgate district.

* * *

The marriage of YB1's eighteen-year-old son in 1930 to a seventeen-year-old woman brought some stability into the fabric dyer's family. Moving into his own residence, the young man and his wife soon established their own businesses. She, daughter of one of Hsinchu's Taoist families, brought into her husband's newly established household on Shui-t'ien Chieh her father's thriving Chinese herbal medicine practice. She also brought the Taoist family shrine, statues of K'ui-hsing (Kuixing) the patron spirit of scholars, Kuanyin (Guanyin) the Bodhisattva of Compassion, and T'ieh-kuai Li (Li Tieguai) one of the Taoist Eight Immortals who carries a gourd filled with medicines for healing. The Taoist tradition of healing was continued by this eldest daughter of an ordained Taoist priest in her husband's household.

The young man, meanwhile, opened a clothes-making business on the first floor of the residence, hiring seamstresses to sew suits and dresses made to order, from cloth produced by his brothers in the fabric dying business, and imported woolen fabric. Together they managed two thriving businesses, while bearing three children, an eldest daughter who inherited the clothes making business, and two sons, one who followed his mother in the Taoist herbal remedy tradition, and the other a photography shop for developing and enlarging pictures. The family flourishes until today, the eldest daughter having expanded the family business into a full clothes production factory, and the younger son (who owns a mansion in the suburbs of the city) a computer generated graphics company along with the photo enlarging business. The second son's modern family flourished without adoptions or concubine liaisons.

***

In all of the above narratives, adoptions were made by one or another member of the family to preserve power, authority, or well-being in the family unit. As Taiwan became more affluent, and the birth of children stabilized, adoptions became less and less frequent. The phenomenon of a concubine (recognition of paternity, in the traditional system) is replaced by divorce in the modern Chinese world, when woman's authority becomes recognized, and rejection of the unfaithful husband possible. But as will be seen, divorce is still considered demeaning to the woman, even in the modern Chinese environment.

In all of the above cases, we believe, the family is seen to be a stabilizing factor in the stresses and failures of human life. No matter what means are used, our informants tell us, family must be maintained as a basic social, economic, and humanly nourishing institution for survival in China.

3. STUDIES OF FAMILIES IN BEIJING, NORTH CHINA
(Family Interviews; *Pinyin* Romanization)

Beijing, China's modern capital, home to emperors from the Mongol Yuan through the Chinese Ming and Manchu Qing dynasties (1281 - 1912), is, at the end of the twentieth century, a city caught in the throes of modernization, gross monetary profit and social-political anomaly. More than one fourth of the population of twelve million plus, that is, about three million are impoverished peasants who have flooded in from the poorer provinces looking for employment, profit, and survival. Called *Waidiren* (outsiders) by long-time Beijing residents, these poorly clad, often unruly and sometimes even lawless elements in Beijing society, collect garbage, repair shoes, build roads, sell vegetables, wait on tables, and do all the tasks that born-and-bred in Beijing citizens, for the most part, dislike.

Another group of non-native Beijing dwellers are the power elite, millionaire entrepreneurs, who drive the most expensive and recent Mercedes-Benz models, wear leather jackets, chain smoke cigarettes, and carry portable phones to extravagant banquets. Long and loud telephone conversations placed during meals are signs of their high social status.

A third group of lesser ranking officials, nouveau-riche and their teenage children, plain clothes PSB policemen, and benighted foreigners patronize Beijing's special kind of nightlife, geared to please any taste that can pay the price. Karaoke and KTV bars, fronts for a burgeoning prostitution trade, discos with teenagers performing amateur jazz and rock style dance on make-shift stages, entertain high paying customers. The gross profit from the nightlife business in Beijing lines the pockets and fills the bank accounts of investors and PSB police officials who allow any business that pays protection money to function without interference.

Office workers on lunch breaks, and the children of Beijing's ordinary residents patronize America's most popular fast food places, with costs equal to or a little less than the fare served in fancy Beijing restaurants. Fast food restaurants appeal to all levels of citizens. They provide convenient places to stop and eat quickly while biking back and forth to work, school, or modern shopping centers. Children of the middle classes bring their parents to Pizza Hut, MacDonalds, KFC, Dunkin Donuts, 31 Flavors, Il Dolce Fredo, A&W Root Beer, TGI Friday's and newer names such as other Kenny Rogers, on holidays.

Concomitant with these manifold signs of economic progress are also to be found discarded plastic wrappers, paper bags, and used lunch boxes, that pollute streams, hang like streamers blowing in tree branches, and further defile a city which takes no pride in its public or private appearance, outside of those areas where state officials and foreigners are driven. The slogan of the recently deceased paramount leader, stated in chapter 1, "To get rich is glorious" is one of the only statement of the government that the citizens of Beijing (and all China, for that matter) take seriously.

With all of these signs of progress has come a dramatic rise in the divorce rate of families in Beijing city. Some 16% of overall marriages, 40% of those in the thirty-to-forty-year-old age group, end in divorce in Beijing. According to statistics gathered by the Ford Foundation supported Women's Crisis center, divorce is highest among white collar working women with college degrees, whose salaries are higher than their husbands'. The source of the divorce comes, statistically, as much from the male side of the household who's authority is threatened and self-esteem lowered, as from extra-marital affairs conducted by one or both money earners in the family.

It is against the background of political bankruptcy, coal and car exhaust pollution, traffic congestion, and intense pressure to earn money in a rapidly expanding economy, that the five families included in this segment of our study live out their lives and survive in contemporary Beijing, China.

The real names of the people interviewed have been changed. Each person of the five Beijing families whose history is recounted, has seen the Chinese and if comprehended, the English version of the manuscript, and approved of its re-telling. Though the histories do not go back further than the war with Japan, the accuracy and reliability of each story transcends in intensity and feeling the statitistical details of the five families from Taiwan, examined in chapter 2.

32

Case 1. Shandong Family, youngest member moved to Beijing.
Interview 1. Sixty-seven-year-old grandmother

The first person interviewed for her story is a 67 year old grandmother, from sturdy peasant stock in Shandong province, to the southeast of Beijing. She speaks with a heavy countryside accent, and like many older women, enjoys smoking a cigarette after meals, and cooking favorite dishes for her "adopted out" daughter and favorite grandson. The interview took place in a sixth floor tenement flat in the *Wudaokou* area of Beijing, site of a late Qing dynasty railroad station, now famous for row-after-row of brick and concrete tenement flats.

"I was seven years old when the Japanese invaded our small village. My husband's father was killed by soldiers, who tore his body apart by pulling him, feet and hands each tied to a horse, in front of the whole village. My mother-in-law was raped, along with most of the women and many girl children of our village. She never recovered from this experience, and died in her mid-sixties, a mad woman. I was brought up by my three elder brothers, and cared for the youngest, a boy child.

"When I was thirteen years old, I was forced to marry a very elderly man who, at that time, was the village Taoist (*tiaoshen*, Shandong dialect, term for a popular Taoist). I hated the old man, and ran away. Following liberation, relatives found my present husband for me. He was a party member, an engineer, and had been put in charge of a state run factory. I had four children by him, first two boys, then two girls.

"During the cultural revolution, our family was separated, not to be joined again fully until the mid 1980's. My two sons were sent to do hard labor, and my husband had to hide in the attic of his factory for two years, from elements in the Party who sought to kill him. We sent food to him late at night, smuggled into his hiding place by friends. My eldest daughter stayed with me, but my second daughter was adopted out as a *yangnü* to a neighboring family. I did not want to lose my second daughter, but was forced to relinquish her, and raised instead a newly born daughter of a relative, who had been sent to work in a distant province during the cultural revolution. The daughter we adopted out lived nearby, so we could visit her frequently.

33

"After the cultural revolution ended, my two sons returned home, married, and took jobs in our town, nearby our family residence. The eldest son became part of a trading company, and eventually went into business for himself. My second son was made vice-president of a woolen cloth weaving factory, the main buyers for which were Japanese and English clothes manufacturers. My eldest daughter worked in a state owned food and grain store, that was closed down by the State austerity program in the 1990's. Her husband works for a state owned firm that is still in operation. His *danwei* (work unit) gives him a Santana (Shanghai-made Volkswagon) to drive. Due to the austerity program in the nineties, our family is now much poorer than it was in the eighties. Only my youngest daughter, who returned to us and took back our family's last name, went to Beijing to college and has a high-paying job that supports us in our needs.

"Each of my children had one child. The oldest son a girl, the second a boy, the eldest daughter a boy, and my own youngest daughter, who returned to our family before entering college, a boy. My adopted daughter also gave birth to one son. In all, I have five grandchildren, one girl and four boys.

"I spend as much of my time as possible with my youngest daughter in Beijing. It was a terrible mistake to let her be adopted out. She hates me for it. But I do my best to help look after their son, since both husband and wife work. I also enjoy Beijing life more than Shandong, because of the way of life, and the good friends I have made here on the college campus where her husband works. I play mahjong everyday, when their son, my grandson, is away at school. He is my favorite grandson, but he is terribly naughty and spoiled. The only way to make him do his homework is to promise to take him to Mac-Donalds." (She laughs as she says this).

Her story was interrupted by the arrival home from school of her grandson. She turned to give him food and drink, then helped him with his homework.

Interview 2. The adopted daughter.　　(Text written in Chinese).

"One of the clearest memories of my life is that I was given away by my parents to another family, when I was 1.5 years old. I knew

34

my family didn't love me. For the rest of my life I would be a guest, first in my adoptive family, then in my own family when I returned from Beijing to visit.

"My adoptive family was very nice to me, always treating me very carefully, like a lodger. I had one older brother, twenty years my senior. He was made manager of a state run wrist watch manufacturing company, so my adoptive family was more wealthy than my real parents were. Our houses were very close, so it was easy to return home and see my real parents if I wanted. But my grandmother, (*nai-nai*, father's mother) who was crazy from the rape of our village by Japanese during the war, would chase me away and not let me enter.

"When I was five years old, playing alone in front of my adoptive parents' home, a neighbor offered to look after me. He put me on the back of his bicycle, and everyday drove me to his place of work, in a school in the countryside. He was a *wushu* martial arts teacher, and each day taught me the traditional Shandong style of martial arts, from the time I was five years old. Our town is very close to Liang Shan, the home of the Song dynasty martial arts heroes who are described in the novel *Shuihu Juan.* Our team competed in local and state competitions. We always won first place.

"When I was twelve years old, the teacher called me forth during a state competition to perform a solo Taiji Sword demonst-ration. Much to my surprise, I was awarded first prize in the overall competition, and a scholarship to train in the Shandong Province Martial Arts Academy. From then on, most of my life was spent in boarding school, coming home only during holidays to visit my adopted and sometimes real family.

"On one of these trips home, I got into a fight with my real older sister. This made my real father very angry. He struck me with his fist, so that I fell down and rolled under the table. I did not fight with him, though I could have bested him. Instead I got up and went back to my adopted home. I could not forget this event for all of my life.

"By the end of my high school training period, I was winning state and national competitions. I decided to take the college entrance exams for a university in Beijing. One night, when I came home from school, I saw that my real parents and my adoptive parents were meeting the front room. I could not help overhearing what they were saying to each other.

"We will let her return to your family," my adoptive father told my real parents, "if she passes the entrance exams into college. If she does not pass, we will keep her in our family and employ her in the watch assembly plant that her older brother manages."

"Hearing their plan was a terrible shock to me. I redoubled my efforts to study, spending most of my time in the school dorm preparing for the exam. I went back to my real family the night before the exam, to see my real mother. She saw how tired I was, and prepared a big dinner for me. We did not tell my father that the next two days were college exams.

"On the way out the door, the next morning, my father said, `There that girl goes, out to play again.' I almost cried, but kept back my tears, more determined than ever to pass the exams, and be admitted to college.

"At noon we were allowed an hour for lunch. I was deeply moved, because my mother was waiting for me outside the classroom. She had carried a hot lunch for me to eat, in between exams. I almost cried again. For both days she looked after me, without telling anybody what I was really doing.

"The results of the exam were posted. I was given a full scholarship to attend the university in Beijing. I continued to train for the national martial arts team, and enrolled for a degree in sports administration and athletic health.

"The night after the exam results were posted, I moved back to my real family. I remember rolling up my bedding and few belongings, and carrying them over my shoulder down the street to my real home. As I crossed the street, I fell in a ditch, and spilled all of my things on the ground. I was so anxious to be in my real home again. That night my mother gave me clean blankets from home, and washed all my dirty things the next day.

"In college I excelled in sports, and made the national team for *Wushu* competition. I won championships each year, in a variety of martial arts skills.

36

"During my third year at college I met and began dating the man whom I was to marry. He was from northeast China, a long distance runner, very tall and handsome. It was not permitted for any of us to have dates or courtship during college. So we met on weekends in parks, far from school. Still, word of our friendship got out. Due to this, I was denied membership in the communist party (I would have refused membership had I been asked), but my husband, who was made a party leader even as a student, always held this against me.

"Also during this time I was sent to Lhasa, and twice to Japan, to demonstrate martial arts techniques. I was also given acting roles in four Hongkong Gongfu movies, playing opposite famous male Kungfu actors.

"Upon graduation I was assigned to teach in a university which did not need or want my martial arts skills, only someone to lead physical exercises early in the morning. This was a very frustrating experience, which many of my classmates also shared. We were not allowed to do the things we were trained for. Instead the departmental chairman assigned us to tasks that were demeaning and unfulfilling. Still, we were not allowed to complain, but were required to obey our elders, in the manner that traditional women were expected to do.

"To be a woman in China is very hard. It becomes more and more a problem, as we move into the twenty-first century. Women hired to work in foreign companies lose the freedom they had while employed in a Chinese firm. The long hours, and dedication expected by the foreign firm hurts life at home.

"After my assignment to a teaching post in a university, I was again offered acting jobs in Hongkong Kungfu movies. But the chairman of our department insisted that all the money I earned should be given to him to distribute as he saw fit. I was not allowed to earn more than my instructor's salary of RMB 400 a month (U.S. $50). Of course I refused to act in any more movies. Instead, I started training students in martial arts, as a hobby. Over a five-year period, I trained 300 students. Of these, six won prizes in national competition. I also accepted many foreign students in my special after-school classes.

"In 1994 I was offered a job by a foreign educational firm. After a year of training in the States, I returned to China to a much more lucrative position, teaching and helping administer language and culture programs. My salary was much higher than my husband's. This is when our troubles began.

"I used my hard-earned salary for many family projects. My elder adopted brother needed a very expensive operation. My parents-in-law also borrowed from my earnings. The biggest expense of all was the purchase of a modern three bedroom flat for our family, on my husband's campus.

"To earn all this money required long hours of work. I often was on duty until late into the night, looking after the needs of the students. My mother came from Shandong to look after our son, with an *a-yi* maid to cook and help him with his homework. My husband often stayed out at night, drinking with party comrades.

"Then one day, shortly after our home was completed, my husband announced that he wanted a divorce. He was having an affair with another woman, whom he wanted to marry. She, too, was married, but had been left by her husband with a single son to care for. I found a lawyer to help me, but was told that according to the law there was nothing I could do. Half of the house legally belonged to my husband, and if we divorced, I would have no place to live.

"Our problem has had a deep effect on our son. He began fighting at school, and his grades went down dramatically. The school principal called me in to express their concern over his behavior. Then last Saturday morning a very special thing happened, which gives some small ray of hope in our family relationship.

"My son wanted to see a movie. I promised to take him, but as we were getting ready, he insisted that his father come with us.

"I can't go," he told our son, "I have something else to do." In fact he was going to see his girl friend and her son.

"My child was adamant. `Papa, you are coming with us!' he insisted.

"Just then the phone rang. It was the son of his lady friend. `I'm sorry, I'm busy today. I won't be able to join you,' he told them.

"When we got to the theatre, our son insisted on sitting between us.

"The movie was about an earthquake, very terrifying for our son to watch. During the screening, he reached over and took my hand. Then he reached over for his father's hand too. He put both of our hands together, holding them there for the rest of the movie.

"This week, our son's behavior improved a little. He joined the Young Pioneers, and wears a red scarf around his neck at school, sign of a new responsibility to work hard and be a good example. For my son's sake, I do not want a divorce. There is no place for a divorced woman to go in China, and I do not want to lose my son."

The divorce of husband and wife was finalized, after the above account was written. The wife was given the son (who chose to be with his mother) and the husband asked the court for and received the house. A small sum of money was paid to the wife, as compensation for the investment she had made in building the three bedroom mansion. She subsequently moved to a rented flat, with her mother and the *a-yi* from Shandong, to look after her son while she works.

Case 2. Divorced woman, PhD in Philosophy, Journalist.

Case #2 is different from all the other narratives in the study, due to the fact that the respondent, a scholar and highly paid journalist, prepared the text herself, in English. I repeat the account here, with a few editorial changes.

"I was born in Hunan province to a high ranking Communist Party family. Both of my parents were officials, busy all the time with meetings and other duties. My younger brother and I were brought up by my mother's parents. We rarely saw our parents when young, but now I see them frequently, especially my father, when he comes to Beijing for Party meetings.

"During my elementary and high school days, I was always very shy, and did not play or associate very closely with my classmates. Instead I spent most of my time studying. I received the highest grades at school. I was two years old when the Cultural Revolution began, and still in High School when it ended.

"Because my grades were so high, it was suggested that I take the entrance exams for Beijing University (*Beida*). I did, and passed with the highest honors. I was accepted into the Philosophy department, and after graduation went on to get an M.A. and Ph.D. I was the first woman to be awarded a Ph.D. degree in modern philosophy at *Beida* (Beijing University), the most prestigious sort of thing that could happen to a woman in modern China.

"During my MA studies I met a handsome young man in our study section. We fell in love, and he proposed to me. I accepted. It was the proper thing to do, I felt, and meant some sense of security and stability for me during studies. Upon receiving our M.A. degrees, we were given an apartment on campus. He began teaching, while I continued my studies for the doctorate.

"Passing my Ph.D. comprehensive exams and writing my thesis were very time consuming. I was unable to fulfill the duties of a house-wife at home. When I finally received my degree and was waiting for my job assignment, I came home one day to find that my husband had a lady friend, with whom he was very intimate. I could not tolerate this situation, and asked for a divorce. He admitted that he was envious of my superior position in the world of learning, and preferred a wife who would be at home, cook, do dishes and wash clothes. He agreed to let me stay in the apartment, since I had nowhere to go. Until this day I reside by myself in a small single room apartment on campus.

"My first job was in a state publishing house, where I was employed as an editor, re-writing innocuous articles by Party motivated scholars with no real interest in intellectual dialogue or other pursuits. During this time I did much research on my own, managing between office duties to publish five books, and a number of scholarly articles. As a result of my publications, I was offered a much more lucrative job in an international press. I applied for post graduate studies in the United States, and was accepted for research there, but still feel more comfortable about living and working in China. I would like to have a baby, to build my own family, if the opportunity comes along. For the present, I must be self-reliant to survive until old age in China."

Case 3. PSB police woman and family.

Police woman Zhao lives in a flat inherited from her father-in-law, in the Wudaokou area of northwest Beijing. It is their second flat, the first being rented out to a Korean woman and her son, where they used to live before her step-mother-in-law retired to an old folk's home, and turned over her deceased husband's apartment to the Zhao family.

Officer Zhao's position in the police department is very influential. It is her responsibility to grant or deny drivers licenses to people who pass the driving lessons and tests required to drive a car or motorcycle in Beijing. Neighbors hold her in great respect, and come asking for favors when their children go before the Haidian Police Office to register for their driver's license. Officer Zhao refuses to take bribes, and lectures the hundred or so traffic officers under her to be strict and honest about giving out tickets for traffic violations.

The Zhaos have one child, a boy, who is in grade school. The boy takes after his father, who is a quiet, soft-spoken police officer in the Criminal Investigation unit. Mrs. Zhao takes her son to school every morning on her bicycle before going to work and comes home at night to cook and look after her husband and son.

The Zhaos were my neighbors and close friends during my two years of residence in the Haidian district. It was due to their influence that I was allowed to live in a Chinese tenement house, with police permission. Each month of the year someone was assigned from one or another doorway opening out into the stairway that led to the sixth floor where I lived, the task of collecting that month's water and electricity money. The Zhaos did this for me, when it was my turn, for which I was very grateful.

The Zhaos are also friends of family case 1 described above. Their sons play together in the apartment garden. Both police officers spent a great deal of time and effort with the estranged husband and wife, hoping they will patch up their differences and stay together.

"Divorce is not a real option, for most Chinese women," Ms. Zhao told me, on one of the mornings that I was getting ready to bike the 14 kilometers to my school work unit. "I know every woman in this tenement flat," she declared, "And there is not one, I assure you, who is totally satisfied with their husband's performance. For a Chinese man, lovemaking is just bang-bang and it's all over. Women can't expect too much from their husbands. Staying together for the sake of one's child is more important than anything else."

Mr. Zhao, who was busy getting his son ready for school, smiled patiently, but did not look up while his wife was talking. "We think they (Case #1) are both very nice people," he said, when she had finished, "And hope they will settle their dispute. Divorce is very hard on the woman in modern China. There is no place for her to go."

Whenever I go off on research trips to Yunnan, Qinghai, or Tibet, the Zhaos look after my birds and flowers. Raising birds and carrying them around in cages is one of the favorite hobbies of Beijing residents. People who raise birds are called *niaoren (bird people)*. It provides a ready means for close contacts with other Beijing families. The Zhaos enjoy looking after my birds when I am away, but are too busy with their work to let their son have his own birds.

As I leave the door each morning, and return at night, the neighbors all greet me. In Beijing, one must use the polite form, "Nin hao" Mrs. Zhao told me, instead of "Ni Hao" used by *Waidiren* (peasants from the provinces) and other southerners, who have flooded into the *Wudaokou* area of Beijing.

Case 4. Waidiren, street sellers of fruit and vegetables.

Just outside my tenement flat is a huge street market, populated by hundreds of *Waidiren*, peasants who have come from distant provinces to earn a slightly higher salary and better way of life in Beijing. The majority of street peddlers are from Anhui and Henan provinces in central China, just north of the Yangtze river. Others, fewer in number, are from such places as Shandong (the coastal province southeast of Beijing) and Hubei (central China), or as far south as Jejiang and Sichuan provinces in southeast and west China.

No matter where they are from, the people in the street markets have a kind of common bond between them, that lets others exist and prosper. Competing businesses open portable shops next to each other, lined up in rows along the streets in front of the Wudaokou apartments. Bargaining for the freshest produce for the lowest price is a serious game that everyone partakes in. The sellers know that I have small birds at home, and give me lettuce, cucumbers, and cabbage leaves for free to feed them.

42

The family that sells vegetables near the street side entrance to our apartments is from Anhui. The father purchased a cart and mule, riding everyday to the outdoor farmer's market on Third Circle Road to buy produce at 4:00 A.M. He is back by 6:30 or so, and opens shop by 7:00 AM when the parents begin walking or biking their children to the school across the street. While he is gone the mother looks after their three children, whom they have brought with them from Anhui, hoping to enroll them in the better Beijing schools. Since it is forbidden for the children of *Waidiren* to attend Beijing's public schools, they have paid extra money to enroll one of their children in the elementary school by the gate.

The other two children are too young, and stay home all day in the lean-to shack erected from discarded wood, tin, and cardboard boxes by the railroad tracks about a mile north of the apartment. Their home is rented from a farming family that still maintains a plot of land for growing vegetables and flowers. The mule stays in a rented lean-to on the farmer's property.

When the mother comes to help the husband, she locks the younger children in their home, with a small black-and-white TV set left on to entertain them. She returns at noon to get their lunch, and if the weather is good, brings them along to play by the cart while she and her husband sell vegetables. She returns home with all three children in the late afternoon, when school is out, to do household chores and get dinner. The father of the family continues to sell vegetables until it is dark, and almost everything is sold. He lets the mule graze in the small, unkempt park in front of the apartments during the day. At night, the mule shares spoiled or left over vegetables with the family.

All of the money earned by the couple, after rent is paid and food supplies purchased, is sent home to their farming family in Anhui. Their aging parents, no longer able to work, live in a large, two story modern house built for the entire extended family by the earnings of the son and daughter-in-law in Beijing. In all, two younger brothers, their wives and children, live with the parents, in the Anhui home built by the couple's earnings. Before coming to Beijing, the family was very poor, with only a mud hut to live in. The farming land they own in

Anhui did not produce enough to support even one family. Now, while the two younger brothers work on the farm, their wives go into a nearby city to work. All of them hope to build their own homes, someday.

While talking with the vegetable sellers from Anhui, neighboring shop keepers also volunteered to tell their family stories. The shop on the corner, who sell grain, (flour, millet, rice, beans, and noodles), household necessities (sugar, salt, canned goods, cigarettes, packaged noodles, other food), are from Henan. Their entire family, two brothers, their wives and the parents, have moved to the little shop in Beijing to live. They sleep in a back room at night, and open shop by 6:00 AM every morning.

Next to them is a small restaurant which sells *youtiao* (which the Taiwanese called *youjiagui*, deep-fried demon, in the Introduction), and other breakfast foods in the morning. It caters to students during the day, and serves inexpensive dinners to apartment residents at night. The name written over the doorway is "Friends of Students Restaurant." It is owned and operated by a couple from Hebei province, (just south of Beijing), who employ a cook from Sichuan and a young waitress from Shandong to do all the work for them.

The name of the seventeen year old girl who waits on tables is "Xiao Hong" (Little red). She and both of her brothers came from a very poor farming area near Liang Shan in Shandong to find employment and wealth in Beijing. The restaurant often stays open until 1:00 or 2:00 A.M., which gives Xiao Hong only three or four hours sleep a night before the owners open shop again in the morning.

If Xiao Hong falls asleep at night or sleeps late in the morning, her pay of ¥400 ($50) a month is docked. Sometimes she is only given ¥250 ($31) or so, due to the stinginess of the proprietress. Xiao Hong sends all of her earnings home to her mother. Her mother doesn't spend the money, she told me, but puts it in the bank instead, as a dowry for her, when she gets married.

All of the neighborhood, the vegetable sellers, grain dealers, and fruit sellers, worried about the health of Xiao Hong. The only reason that the restaurant was so successful, everyone agreed, was due to Xiao Hong's personality. She looked after school children, knew most of the customers by name, and faithfully stayed up until the wee hours looking after late-night drinkers and revelers.

It was due to one of these late-night parties that the neighborhood got together and found a better place of employment for Xiao Hong. Just past midnight a large black car pulled up, with leather-coated portable phone-carrying businessmen. (The car, a late model Audi, had a *Jia* or military license plate). They entered the restaurant, ordered beer, then called for Xiao Hong to sit at their table. They were the owners of a highly profitable business, a disco and karaoke bar by the Jishuitan bridge near Second Circle road in Beijing, they told her. They had come to offer her a job as a waitress and dancer in their club.

Xiao Hong, of course, strongly objected, claiming her conservative Shandong origins as the best of all reasons to refuse, no matter what the salary, to work in a bar.

The entire neighborhood took offense at the effrontery of the *Jia* license-plated, leather-coated mafioso, to even suggest corrupting an innocent *Waidiren* from Shandong. A restaurant just down the street, inside the gates of a nearby university, offered her a job with a room and better salary. Xiao Hong now works regular hours, 10:00 AM to 10:00 PM. The vegetable sellers, grain dealers, and streetside merchants feel they must help each other, like an extended family, to survive in Beijing.

Case 5. Mathematics professor, Four-walled Mansion (Sihoyuar).

The fifth respondent included in the Beijing segment of the study is one of two long time Beijing residents chosen to relate his family story. The entire account, were it to be retold, would rival in length and complexity Jung Chang's *Wild Swans*, (London: 1992), which is itself one of the most moving and graphic descriptions available in print of a Chinese family history lasting through three generations of violent change in China. A majority of Chinese families have similar tales of suffering and family caring.

Professor Zhou (not his real name) was born to intellectual parents in one of Beijing's oldest and most distinguished *Sihoyuar* (Four-wall garden) mansions. The residence, near the old Confucian temple, just west of the Yonghegong temple, was assigned them during the Daoguang reign years, (ca. 1830), and remained in their possession until the Cultural Revolution.

Zhou's mother, a Ph.D. in mathematics, had rented a set of rooms from her parents, to house her scholar husband, and later their only child, during the difficult years of study for their doctorates. After the establishing of the People's Republic in 1949, her parents and their entire family were forced to move out from the huge mansion. By some stroke of luck, the Party and City authorities decided that the daughter, with her husband and child, could remain in their small three-room segment of the mansion, since technically they were not landlords, but renters. The rest of the family mansion was turned into quarters for Liberation Army generals. Zhou grew up in this quiet, "old Beijing" environment.

Today five other families reside in the old *Sihoyuar* mansion, filling the former gardens and servants' quarters with ugly brick shanties, clothes lines, and makeshift apartments. Like so many other *Sihoyuar* in old Beijing, only the roofs and doorways of the old mansion give evidence of the cultured way of life hidden behind the decorated walls and stone carvings of the past.

Zhou's parents were employed in the former Fu Jen University Science and Math department, which was changed to the *Shifan* Normal University campus after liberation. Both parents were respected scholars. During the cultural revolution, they were targeted for punishment. Along with the downgrading of professors and educators were the aggravating circumstances of their landlord past.

Though neither of Zhou's parents were Christian, they had received their degrees from the old Catholic University of Fu Jen. Both parents were arrested, subjected to degrading meetings, and beaten. Due to the immense stress, both contracted cancer. Since they were from the wrong political class, no hospital would accept them for treatment.

Young Zhou, now solely responsible for the well-being of his parents, tried to think of the best way to help them. He went to work in a chemical factory, and seriously burned his hands from overwork in production. (The scars on his knuckles are still visible today).

46

By some stroke of good luck, he was considered a worker hero, and was invited to join the Party. He soon became a zealous, patriotic member, and was promoted to a leadership position in the factory. Only then was it possible to get medical treatment for his parents. But by then it was too late.

As he watched his parents die from the ravages of cancer, Zhou spent his free moments studying mathematics with his mother, and reading literature with his father. He became a self-made mathematician, and a scholar on the social background and history of the *Dream of the Red Chamber*, a novel about a high-ranking mid-Qing dynasty family. He did not marry at this time, but dedicated himself to looking after his parents, getting them medication, and finally seeing to their burial.

After the Cultural Revolution ended, Zhou went back to college and received an MA in mathematics. He married a woman from Beijing, and brought her to dwell in the three rooms in the old *Sihoyuar* mansion, which were still in his possession. He was soon given a job in a science oriented university, and was overjoyed when his wife gave birth to a daughter. "If I had a son, I would beat him, like Bao Yü's father beat him in the *Dream of the Red Chamber*," he declared. "But since she is my daughter, I shall treat her with respect and dignity."

Zhou and his wife both work, earning enough to send their daughter to one of Beijing's best high schools. The daughter is a gifted violinist. Zhou hopes that one day she will be able to go to the Julliard school in the States to study.

The wealth of detail provided by the household registers of Hsinchu city cannot be reduplicated for the five families interviewed in Beijing. It is possible to piece together the history of each family, from the present back to the grandparent's generation. Even though the uxorilocal marriage and the child bride adoption *(tongyangxi)* are no longer present in official Beijing city registers, in fact many of the young couples working in Beijing must live with their in-laws due to the lack of housing.

In many of the cases interviewed, not included in the narratives above, the husband lives with his wife's parents, who provide a home for their son-in-law and baby-sit their daughter's child, while both work.

47

The rules of the past which made living with agnatic in-laws (uxorilocal husband) less desirable, are now a practical solution in modern Beijing. The new, practical grand family provides, at one-and-the-same time, care for the elderly, a baby-sitter for son or daughter, and a residential apartment in modern Beijing.

Margery Wolf's *Revolution Postponed* (Stanford, 1985: 221-237) gives many telling examples of rural domestic problems while the work brigade system was still in operation. Changes which have occurred after 1989 make much of the work done by authors in the late seventies and early eighties in need of re-telling. Many of the families interviewed in Beijing prefer a daughter rather than a son to look after elderly parents. Younger wives look to their mothers to come and baby-sit their children, instead of their husband's mother. In many affluent Beijing families women earn as much or more than their husbands, making it all the more necessary either to have a grandparent living with the family, hire an *a-yi* maid, or put the only child into an expensive private school which provides after-school care, while both of the parents work. The evidence from the Beijing families interviewed shows clearly that life after work centers on the family and the social as well as financial security it provides its members.

4. CASE STUDIES OF MINORITY FAMILIES IN CHINA

Perhaps the most striking thing about living in China is its overwhelming population, spread out over a vast area of land that is for the most part barren and inhospitable for farming. The peasants of the north China plain eke out a harsh living from brown fields that depend on summer thunder-and-lightning storms for sufficient water to plant and reap a harvest. The Yellow River, in its upper reaches (the Qinghai province highlands) flows swiftly through incredibly beautiful gorges, carrying loess silt to the dry plains below. These highlands are known in Tibetan as Amdo, a land inhabited by Goluk, Maqu, Sogko, and other peoples speaking dialects of Tibetan different from Lhasa.

As it curves northward into the Gobi desert of Islamic Ningxia and the grasslands of Inner Mongolia, the Yellow River becomes sluggish and slow. By the time it turns eastward again and pours out into the north China plain, there is not enough strength left to supply all of north China's wheat and vegetable farmers with enough water for irrigation and daily living. From the upper source of the Yellow River we have chosen two minority families, one Tibetan and one Islamic Hui, to include in the anecdotal section of our study.

The inland province of Yunnan in the southwest is one of the most underdeveloped and culturally unchanged areas of China. The reasons for this isolation are, first, the outlying areas of greater China have poor roads, making them difficult to access for development or commercial trade. Second, the provinces of southwest and west China are for the most part inhabited by China's minorities, i.e., non-Han people. Unlike the United States and other western nations, the minorities of greater China may choose to keep their culture and language somewhat intact.

From this area we have chosen families from two minority groups, the Aini-Hani and the Muosuo, to include in the study. These families and cultural groups were chosen because they have managed to keep their customs and way of life (and language) more-or-less intact from Han influence. In these remote areas, as we will see, the family is also the basis for cultural, economic, and social survival.

Case 1. A Tibetan Family in Qinghai

The source of the Yellow River in the highlands of central Qinghai Province is one of the most beautiful and unexploited areas in China. A thirty-two-hour ride by train from Beijing to Lanzhou, followed by a seven-hour bus to the village of Xiaho, in south Gansu, brings one to the boundary of this vast area that is known in Tibetan as Amdo. Four kinds of Tibetan people in Amdo patronize the great temple of Labrang, built in Xiaho in the year 1706-10 by the King of Sogko. (Xiaho means "clear water" in Amdo dialect). These four kinds of people are the Amdo and Mongol speaking group of the Kingdom of Sogko, the Goluk nomads from the higher grasslands surrounding Mt. Animachin and the Bayankarla pass, the Maqu nomads of Qinghai and south Gansu, and the people of nearby Joni, an area the Han Chinese have named *Hezuo*, cooperation.

Kamba nomads from west Szechuan, and from Yüshu (Jegundo) in southeast Qinghai, also come to the Labrang temple on pilgrimage. Labrang is now the largest Yellow Hat (Gelugpa, Dalai Lama sect) temple in greater Tibet, with some 1,500 monks in residence, 900 permanent monastics, and 600 students from other temples in the Amdo and Kham regions.

For the reader unfamiliar with the linguistic geography of Tibet, before and after the Qing dynasty rule (1644-1911) and after Chinese Army control (1950-1959), Tibet is composed of three great regions: Tibet proper, Kham, and Amdo. Tibet is divided into many lesser districts, the most important of which are Lhasa, Shigatse, and Ngari (Ari) in the far west. Ngari is famous for sacred Mt. Kailash.

The area of Kham, part of which appears on KMT (pre-1949) maps as Xikang (Hsi-k'ang), comprises west Szechuan province (all of the area westward from Chengdu), north Yunnan, the northeast tip of Tibet proper (Chamdo), and the southeast tip of Qinghai province, the area of Yüshu (Tibetan, Jegundo).

Amdo, famous for its holy Tibetan monks, including the present Dalai Lama and the recently deceased Panchen Lama, was gerrymandered during the Qing dynasty into Qinghai Province, southern Gansu Province, and the district of Aba in west Szechuan. The dialects of Amdo are the most varied of all Tibet, and the most difficult to learn and understand. People from Kham and Lhasa can mutually understand each other, but Amdo-speaking nomads often need a translator to know what Khamba or Lhasa folk are saying.

The famous botanist and National Geographic explorer Joseph Rock was intimidated by the Goluk area, and brought along a troop of fifty Nakhi militia, a minority people from north Yunnan, to guard him on his plant gathering expeditions into Amdo. The equally famous Alexandra David-Neel, who finally settled down in the temple of Taer-si (Kumbun) near Xining in Qinghai, wrote of her fear of the Khamba, whom she tried to avoid during her travels in turn-of-the century Tibet. Today the areas they traversed are for the most part quite safe. It is from this area that we choose our Tibetan family. Due to the nature of the account, the true identity is disguised by altering the names and places described by the narrator. For the sake of our story, we shall call him Pema.

Pema was born to a nomad family in Amdo. For most of their history, the people of the high plains and mountains had considered themselves an independent kingdom, neither a part of China or Tibet. When the Chinese army came in the early 1950's Pema's family learned for the first time of electric light bulbs ("needles can be found at night," they called light bulbs) and candy. "Don't eat the candy," the wise elders told the children, "It will make you into slaves of the soldiers."

The truth of the elders' statement was quickly brought home to them. The army soon came in numbers, and fought a pitched battle with nomad warriors. Five thousand nomads and their families were killed, but 1,500 soldiers perished with them. From that time on, the kingdom was aware that it was a part of China.

Pema was sent by his family to a monastery in Amdo, where he remained until early 1958, when the soldiers came again to establish Han supervision over the monks. Seven hundred of the older generation of Lamas were executed, Pema and the older monks remember, and the rest vacated the monastery until things quieted down. With two other teenage monks he fled the holocaust, walking all the way to Lhasa.

The trip by foot took ten months to accomplish. When the three arrived, towards the end of 1958, they went at first to Ganden monastery, a three hour bus ride to the east of Lhasa, where Zongkapa, the founder of the Gelugpa school long ago (fourteenth century) established the Yellow Hat (Dalai Lama) Buddhist order. Shortly after Pema's arrival, the Chinese armies entered Lhasa. Word reached the monks of Ganden that the life of the Dalai Lama was in danger. Pema with a group of four other young monks went to Lhasa, to protect the Dalai Lama from harm.

The night before the shelling of Lhasa began, the five young monks went with Dalai Lama as an escort over the Himalayas to Nepal and India. Dalai Lama went on ahead, as they approached the border pass. The young monks with groups of armed Khamba nomads, stayed behind as a diversion. They were given machine guns and other weapons to distract the Chinese soldiers. Planes flying overhead soon spotted them, and a battle ensued. The other four young men, injured in the fighting, were unable to continue. But Pema, with a band of Khamba, made it across the pass and eventually arrived in Dharamsala, to work for the Dalai Lama. There were five bullet holes in his nomad robes from the battle. "Bad shots, those soldiers," he said.

For twelve years Pema worked in Dharamsala and other parts of India. He was sent to Switzerland to gather funds for building a new Sera monastery in India.

Shortly after the monastery was built, Pema met the young woman who was to be his wife. She, too, was from Kham/Amdo, and had come with her family via Katmandu to India. They married, and he was made a teacher (*Gegenla*) in a local Tibetan school. His wife gave birth to two children, a boy, then a girl. As the children began to grow up in India, with modern music, worldly ways, and other emoluments that destroyed the cultural elements of Tibetan life that Pema cherished so dearly, he and his wife made the decision to return to China, to rebuild a home in the highlands.

The government of China was delighted with his decision. Pema and his family were welcomed back. He was offered a high-ranking position teaching in a local high school. They returned via the Katmandu Highway, and stopped for some months in Lhasa. While there, he and other friends returned to Ganden, and helped carry stones back up to the side of the mountain to restore the temple, still in ruins from Chinese army artillery shelling. They also stopped in the original Sera monastery, which also was under repairs, where three hundred or so young students were being trained by older Gelugpa masters. When they arrived home, his wife and children became ill from altitude sickness. It took them a whole year to get used to the highland life.

Following in the footsteps of his father, Pema's son became a monk in a Gelugpa monastery. His daughter enrolled in a prestigious university, and majored in English. Both children vowed to help their parents build a home that equaled the more luxurious way of life they had in India.

The pay of a professor was very little, and Pema was getting older. Instead of going to the United States to study for an M.A., the daughter returned to her highland home, to take over the teaching position of her father, so that he could retire. The son, who had managed to construct a very beautiful and prayerful retreat in the monastic quarters from the stipends he had earned by praying and other monastic ritual, decided to sell his monastic residence, and use the money to build his father a comfortable residence. Between the earnings of the daughter, and the sale of the monk son's meditation and temple-residence, the children helped their father and mother complete their long dreamed for home in the highlands.

Pema's wife, a gentle and loving person, and Pema himself, declare that they cherish their children more than any possession. Even after retirement, Pema remains a true leader in the community. His presence in the local school as a senior professor, is a convincing factor in the lives of the nomad children who come to study. Only by education, learning language, science, and practical skills, he lectures his students, can Tibetans better their way of life in a society that belittles their culture. It is important to go abroad to gain an understanding of how the rest of the world lives. But it is even more important to return in order to preserve all that is good about Tibetan culture, he tells them.

Nomad relatives from his family and that of his wife crowd into their beautiful home on festivals, sleeping everywhere on floors, couches, and beds, warming themselves by the small yak-dung and coal burning stove, eating home roasted bread, zampa with dri (yak) butter, sugar, tea and dried cheese, slices of boiled beef and lamb, and buttered rice mixed with Joma root seasoning. The way of life in the highlands is exhilarating. Monks returning from Dharamsala in India bring news of Buddhist studies and philosophy lectures, the choosing of living Buddhas for temples in Amdo and Kham, and the building of new monasteries. The cultural revival and survival of Tibet in China is assured by the thousands of educators like Pema, for whom extended family and its religious-cultural way of life are primary and crucial.

Case 2. Hani-Aini Life in Yunnan

One of the least known and best preserved cultures of southwest China, the Burma-Laos border, and north Thailand is the Hani-Aini-Akka complex of ethnic peoples. Speaking a Tibeto-Burmese language with religious and cultural roots in pre-historic Bon and popular Taoist ritual, the Aini of Xishuangbana, the Hani of the Red River area, Yunnan, and the Akka of the Golden Triangle (Burma-Laos-Thai) preserve intact a way of life totally oriented around the stem and grand family and the bringing up of children, in remote, inaccessible areas of southwest China.

Whereas neighboring Thai (Dai) tribes who occupy the wet rice growing lowlands converted long ago to Theravada Buddhism, the Aini, who live on and cultivate the hillsides, preserve a cultural-ritual system with deep roots in a shamanistic past, overlaid with yinyang cosmology and a deep respect for the phenomena of nature.

The details of family life recounted here are told in the words of an Aini scholar, who is from a village near the Burma-Laos border, in the south west part of Yunnan. Since family and local customs differ throughout China, the details described here may differ for nearby villages. In whatever way the details may differ, the rapporteur tells us, Aini/Akka family life is everywhere the focus of ritual, social, and festive custom.

"The names given Aini children during childhood affirm the central role of family in daily life. My siblings refer to themselves not by given names, but as older, second, or third brother, older, second, or third sister. When addressed by other villagers, peer groups and teachers may use our given names, but always refer to our parents Xiao-er's mother or Ziran's Father. Sibling rank, rather than given names are used in the family, and with neighboring and village friends. Thus children grow up without using the maiden name of their mother, or her relatives, referring to them as mother's older brother, mother's second younger sister, and so forth.

"The New Year is celebrated by most Aini and Akka villages from the time that special white colored flowers bloom in the mountain highlands. This date usually occurs shortly after the solar New Year, between 2-4 of January. All Aini return home for the celebration, whether working in nearby Jinghong, (Xishuangbana) or far away in Beijing. The new year celebration is a time for family feasting, shared with the entire village. Each family lays out a bountiful banquet table in front of the family house. All of the villagers pass by each house, sampling the delicacies, and enjoying the festival with fellow villagers.

"By the entrance of each village is laid aside a special ritual place for warding off evil, and playing special games which protect, and symbolize (demonstrate) the health and welfare of village children. A swing, teeter-totter, and a pole erected firmly in the ground with a revolving beam on top, like a two-armed merry-go-round, provide village entertainment during the New Year festival.

"Courtship and marriage, like many areas of southeast Asia, is carried out in a small room or house built separately from the family residence. Nubescent girls in their teens are allowed to live in these rooms until they have selected a mate. Once chosen, the boy and girl report their choice to their respective families. The decision for or against marriage is a family rather than individual choice. The parents of both sides must approve the family liaison. Courtship, on the other hand, is left to the boy and girl, lovemaking and intimacy being considered a private matter which the parents should not see or be involved in. Even the watching of love scenes on the ubiquitous television is considered an intrusion of family privacy. I have seen families change channels when love scenes appear on the screen.

"Once married, the boy and girl are given a room in the parents' home, to raise their own children. Rooms are allotted according to status, the father and mother (or grandmother and grandfather, as the case may be) receive the largest room off the main living area, and the eldest, second eldest married son, adjacent rooms. Children may live on the (raised) ground floor, or in second floor bedrooms. Rooms and small dwellings may be added to the residence for the newly weds and their family, and for the courtship of nubescent females.

"The Aini are especially concerned about the death and dying process, and proper burial for a deceased member of the family. It is considered very bad luck if a family member dies away from the ancestral home, the hearth, and family shrine. Full funeral rites cannot be provided unless the person going into the next life does so from the access point within the family household.

"As the moment of death approaches, the whole family gathers around the bedside, as a form of support and "love" (ai) for the dying person. Death, the Aini say, occurs in two ways: "from the feet upward (the dying person can still talk during the process), or from the head down (the dying person has become unconscious).

"Our family was lucky, because our mother died from the feet upward. We all gathered around her bed, to wish her well, holding hands and talking with her. The day she passed away the weather was very clear and placid. The skies were blue, as if heaven had welcomed her into a new home. The villagers all came for the procession. We carried her remains into the hills to the place where our family members are interred. As we got there, the sky began to darken. After the burial, a wind arose, and we all hurried home. That night a huge thunder and lightning storm brought heavy rain and winds. But the next morning, all was clear again. The whole village said:

Your mother was a very great person.

Even heaven cried, when she was buried.

Each year (1993-1997), I try to bring my Beijing language students to visit the minority areas of Yunnan, especially the Aini and the Muosuo, during the Chinese New Year festival. For all of them, as for myself, the experience is truly meaningful. Even though the way of life is primitive, the amenities of modern living such as electricity, showers, and restaurants missing, the peace and warmth of Muosuo and Aini family life make all other considerations seem less important.

The strongest factors working against this cultural tranquility is tourism. The hordes of visiting Hongkong, Taiwan, and overseas Chinese, foreigners and mainland Chinese vacationers, bring with them plastic wrappers, fast foods, film, tourist buses, the need for showers and TV, that are far more effective elements of change than government plans for mandarin language education and police law enforcement. If Muosuo matriarchy and Aini family courtship can survive these economic pressures for modernization, their way of life is perhaps preservable.

Case 3. Muosuo Matriarchy

A journey by bus three days and nights from Kunming northward to the Yunnan-Tibet-Szechuan border brings the persistent traveler-scholar to one of the last remaining matriarchies in the modern world. Not noticed by the Chinese until 1937 (mainly due to the efforts of Joseph Rock, University of Hawai'i Botanist and National Geographic scholar), the Chinese government until today classifies the Muosuo with the more widely known Nakhi people, a day's travel over an 12,000 ft. pass to the south and west of sacred lake Luguhu of the Muosuo. Though the Nakhi are also sometimes called matriarchal, their social life, stature, and ethnic costume are totally unlike the taller, infinitely more isolated Muosuo.

The Nakhi, shorter in stature, were once members of a powerful Kingdom unconquered by the Han Chinese, until the Mongol armies of Kubilai Khan passed by and subdued them. Along with the Nakhi, the Bai, Yi, Pumi and other Yunnan peoples of the Nanchao Kingdom, they became a part of the Yuan or Mongol dynastic rule, remaining more or less a part of the Ming and Qing dynasty legacy without serious interference until the coming of the PLA armies in the 1950's, and the imposition of Marxist-Socialist rule.

The Muosuo, on the other hand, escaped the notice of Kubilai Khan and all Chinese rulers until the coming of the PLA in the 1950's. During the Great Cultural Revolution, zealous Han Red Guard forced the Muosuo matriarchs to declare themselves a patriarchy, and live in the same household as their husbands. At the end of the cultural revolution, however, the villages around sacred lake

Luguhu reverted to original custom. Husbands went home to their mother's family; the true matriarchal, matrilocal, matrilineal society of the Muosuo was restored to its original vigor. It continues so until today, influencing neighboring Pumi and sometimes even the warlike Yi (who occasionally choose to live by the lake side) to accept its matriarchal system.

And, indeed, the Muosuo are a true matriarchal society. The woman who is head of the household owns the land, keeps and raises the children, and passes on the land and family headship rights to a daughter of her choice. The matriarch's elder or younger brother has the position of male authority over the children, ploughs the fields, and sees to the construction and maintenance of the family residence.

The man whom the woman (matriarch or other) chooses to be the father of her child/children, after a period of courtship, may only come at night to sleep with her after the family has retired, and must return home to his mother or sister's family before sunrise. There is a social taboo, in Muosuo matriarchy, for the father of a child to be seen coming or going to his wife's home. One may not ask "who is the father," (as so many rude and untrained anthropologists have done, both Chinese and foreign), but may wait unobtrusively to be introduced, by the matriarch, to the man who is her father or lover. One may also meet the father of a boy or girl of the village during the New Year and other festivals, when custom demands that a child bring gifts or greetings to the paternal ancestor. Otherwise the Muosuo hide the truth of their love life from prying researchers, telling tall stories to Han and other anthropologists.

I first learned of the Muosuo in 1991-92 from scholars at the Chinese Academy of Social Sciences. I was especially impressed by the works of Prof. Song, and a young woman researcher from the Yunnan Social Science publishing house named Dang Ying. Both had published significantly on the Muosuo matriarchy, but had conflicting opinions about their mores and way of life. Song's studies ranged all the way from Muli and the Muosuo of Szechuan across the lake, to the mixed ethnic areas of Yongning (20 kilometers away over a lesser pass) and Ninglang (72 kilometers away, over a 12,000 ft. pass). Dang Ying's studies were conducted mainly in the lakeside village of Luguhu, where matriarchy was in full evidence, and Han influence almost unknown. "There is no Danwei here," (no official Han government office), according to the Muosuo's own account of their lake side village.

Both of these scholars approached the Muosuo with the ethnic bias of the Han Chinese, believing matriarchy to be a proof for the validity of the Marxist "Primitive Law" theory of evolution. Their, and other foreign scholars view of the Muosuo was one of mild shock and scandal, concerning the freedom of the Muosuo woman to choose a man as a father for her child. This view of presumed promiscuity was true not only of scholars who conducted embarrassing question-and-answer style research by the Muosuo firesides, (which I have watched, with great alarm) but also by drunken PSB and other tourist types who drive into the village expecting to find a Muosuo woman to sleep with for the night.

Due to my long association with the village, from January 1993 until the present, I have chosen to leave out any citation of other scholars' findings, hoping rather to let the words and actions of the Muosuo speak for themselves. I hope by so doing to leave behind any bias or cultural judgment about matriarchal women and their close knit, affectionate, and extremely human family relations, leaving the reader to vicariously enjoy the peace and tranquility of a village that has lived for 800 years without war, rape, or violence of any kind, except what was imposed from outside, by Chinese, Yi, or other non-Muosuo forces.

My first view of Lake Luguhu, as with so many other travelers, was through the green pines and snow clad cliffs that lead over the 12,000 ft. pass into the 8,300 ft high lake that has been home of the Muosuo for about 800 years. Our bus carried nine tired and disgruntled American students, a half-Pumi-half-Muosuo woman guide, a Bai bus conductor, and a cranky Han driver who kept adding oil to the differential of the Chinese-made bus every two hours or so, hoping thereby to exact more pay for his services.

It was night time, the road was frozen, and patches of snow made the way slippery. It was a few days before the Chinese new year. The moon was small, and the village without lights (electricity was introduced only two years before this writing). The headlights of the bus showed the lake to be quite large. A huge mountain, called "Lion

Head," the guide told us, could be seen silhouetted against the sky to the west of the lake. We drove along a dirt road, and came to a plank gateway that was lowered by hand so the bus could pass through.

As we pulled into the courtyard, a young woman in her late twenties came out to meet us. Her name was Tsering Joma, a Tibetan name, though she was Muosuo. A dinner around the open Muosuo hearth was waiting for us, after which the women students were given beds in the women's quarters, and almost everyone turned in for the night.

My assigned bed, next to the Buddhist altar, was too cold to climb into. So I went back to warm myself by the fire. Tsering Joma was there, along with four other women of varying ages, and a one-year- old female child. The matriarch, Great-grandmother of the family ("Eje" in Muosuo) motioned me to sit by the right of the fire, while she sat to the far left. Between us was the family altar, directly behind the fire. The altar was in three layers, a lower platform nearest to the flames, a second level with an incense burner, and a third level with a crude adobe clay statue of the Buddha. Around the fire, to my immediate left, were Tsering Joma, her child, a maid named "Barr" (the "r" sound was rolled), Tsering's mother (the child's grandmother), and the great-grandmother. In all there were four generations around the fire, all (except for Barr) either matriarchs or someday to be matriarchs of the family.

Having been in China for many years, I know (by now) not to ask any questions. I sat still, and watched the flames burn in varying shades of yellow, red, green and blue, as the fresh pine wood crackled. Great-grandmother pulled a small teapot out of the fire, in which tea leaves had been boiling furiously. She poured some of this strong tea into a small porcelain cup, mixed in some salt, stirred it with a small juniper branch, and handed it to me. I let it sit for a moment (too hot to sip), then appreciated its flavor, a smoky brick tea such as Tibetans, Mongols, Uighurs, and Khazaks drink. It was the saltiest tea I had ever tasted.

"Salt is a great delicacy for us," Tsering Joma began the conversation. "After the cultural revolution we were so poor that we couldn't afford it. Now that tourists come to Luguhu, we can afford salt, to preserve meat, and put in tea." The next morning Tsering's words were proven true. Three pigs were slaughtered, their bones removed, and the bodies filed with salt. Like huge sausages, the salted whole pigs were put in the loft to dry and become food offerings for the next New Year festival.

"The difference between us and the wild Yi tribes," she continued, "who were brigands and used to rob our village, is that they never learned how to preserve meat. They kill and eat the animal immediately, having nothing left for winter." She pointed to the rafters behind us, the whole back area of the main living room, behind the open hearth.

Inflated pig and cow stomachs (used to store yak/dri butter), dried sausages, salted and dried sides of beef, pork, and a whole salted goose, were hanging from the rafters. Great-grandmother said something in Muosuo, and pointed to what looked like pillowed benches behind us. I squinted in the darkness, and saw what was indeed whole pigs, salted and stacked, on their backs, in rows, awaiting some sort of celebration or banquet.

The servant girl Barr picked up the child, and strapped her to her back, while Tsering was talking. She went to the table at the back of the room, under the dried pig stomachs and sausages, and began to mix a batter of leavened dough for tomorrow's breakfast. The women were talking, so I watched Barr working, then glanced back at the fire.

"Do your students like steamed *momo* (dumplings), fried bread, or roast potatoes for breakfast?" Tsering turned and asked me.

"Don't worry about us, they'll be glad to eat anything you give them," I answered. "The young are always hungry, and we're all delighted to be here."

Dang Ying had warned me never to ask about the father of the child. It was a terrible breach of propriety to ask who a child's father is, in a matriarchal society. It came as a surprise, then, when Eze (Great grandmother) asked me "Do you have any children?" (She knew enough mandarin to ask simple questions).

"Yes, I have two," I said, and took their pictures out of my wallet to show them. "Their names are Theresa and Mari." The pictures were passed all around the room. Great-grandmother, grandmother,

Tsering, and Barr with flour on her hands all examined them, and then passed them back to me.

"They look Asian," Tsering remarked.

"Their mother was Japanese," I answered, "But she left us long ago. I brought them up as a single father."

"They're lovely," they all agreed. "Bring them here next time you come."

I did not stay much longer around the fire, but reluctantly left the women chatting happily, lest my welcome should wear out. "Be sure and come back early, before sunrise," Tsering said. "You can watch the morning prayers by the fireside, and go outside to see the offerings to the mother goddess of the lake."

I slept soundly, the strong tea keeping me warm but not sleepless. The crow of a rooster awoke me. It was still dark, with the first hint of dawn lighting the sky over the east side of the lake. It was slightly cold, just below freezing. I went quickly to the fireside, where Barr was stoking the fire, coaxing the flames to warm the room and the pot of tea set on the coals to boil. She put a large pot of potatoes on the fire to cook, then rolled out the *momo* from the risen flour, laying these over the potatoes to steam for breakfast.

In a short while Great-grandmother awoke, from a bed to the left of the fireplace. She had gone to sleep in her Muosuo clothes, dark grey skirt, red velvet blouse, headdress with large pearls, which she adjusted on her head as she awoke. She donned a yak-hair vest, against the morning chill, and sat to the left of the fire, across from my guest seat to the right.

The grandmother (Tsering's mother) came in next, with a great bundle of juniper branches, which she lit in the fire. One twig of burning juniper was broken off, and put into the incense pot on the altar. To the offering was added a teaspoon of zampa (highland roasted and ground barley). She then went out the door of the household to perform another part of the morning ritual. Barr motioned me to follow.

It was brighter outside, but still before sunrise. Grandmother carried the juniper to an altar shaped like a small stove, with two openings and a chimney. The lower opening held juniper branches and kindling. The upper aperture was a small furnace connected to the chimney. The altar was almost identical both in function and structure to those placed on the roofs of houses in Lhasa, except that the Muosuo altar was placed on the ground, and was meant "to offer sacrifice solely to the mother goddess of the lake and the soil." This is what Tsering told me, as I stood watching Grandmother light the juniper branches in the opening and stoke the fire with several teaspoons of zampa flour.

Tsering led me back into the main room and invited me to sit again by the fire. This time I was made to sit to the left of the fire, next to Great-grandmother.

"The right side of the fire is for guests," she said, "but Eje wants you to sit on the family side this morning. We'll let your students sit over there, around the tables, while you sit here as one of the elders."

I almost blurted out "father figure," but said instead, "you mean, their teacher; sometimes I wonder if I really am the person in authority. American female students are themselves a matriarchy."

"For us, my older brother and mother's uncles are the authorities over our children. The children respect them and do whatever they say." (Yes, it is a true matriarchy I thought, recalling the work of Raymond Firth, *We, The Tikopians*, who had been a wonderful and unassuming mentor at London University. I felt very proud of myself at this moment, but there was much more to learn).

Barr had begun rolling out thick pancake-size bread, and deep-frying them over a second stove to the rear of the room. The tripod over the main hearth fire had meanwhile served as a frame for cooking the potatoes, steaming the *momo*, and then boiling a huge kettle of water. When the water was boiling furiously, grandmother took it off the flames, emptied it into a large teapot with tea leaves inside, then poured the strong brick tea into a Tibetan style tea churn, that looked very much like the old style butter churns used in north Europe. To the tea was added milk, yak/dri butter, and salt.

The mixture was then churned vigorously, and poured back into the large pitcher. A second batch was made, this time with sugar added instead of salt. The yak butter tea with sugar was put into a second pitcher. Now breakfast was ready to be served. Boiled potatoes, steamed *momo*, fried flat bread, and cups of salted or sweet butter tea were served to each person around the fire.

At this moment the men began to come into the room. There were three men that first morning: Great-grandmother's younger brother, a man in his seventies; Tsering's older brother, who was definitely the male authority figure of the family, and a tall, rather thin man in a blue coat and Russia soldier's hat with floppy ear muffs. He was introduced to me as "Gehnge" (pronounced like "uh" in "upper"). All three men were very friendly, and we soon struck up a lively conversation. Gehnge invited me to come with him to the family Buddhist altar, which was upstairs on the second floor of the old family structure, next to the rooms reserved for young unwed women where my students were still sleeping.

I left my breakfast unfinished, and went with Gehnge to the Buddhist altar. It was kept in a room with an outer balcony, facing west (the sacred mountain). Outside the altar was an oil painting of the holy ascetic-poet Milarepa. Inside the door could be seen a traditional Tibetan style altar, with statues of Zongkapa (Founder of the Yellow Hat Gelugpa order), Chenrezig (*Spyan-ras-gzigs, Avalovitesvara*), Manjusri, and White Tara. Various inexpensive Thanka hung from the walls, and a complete set of the Tanjur-Kanjur Buddhist scriptures was stored to the right of the entrance. Gehnge was very devout, pressing his head to the floor at least thirty times, then refilling all of the hundred or so small brass bowls on the altar with water. He chanted a rather short sutra in Tibetan, bowed a number of more times, lit incense, and motioned me that the morning prayer was over. We went back to the main room, took our places by the fire, and finished breakfast. When we were done, Gehnge and Granduncle went out for their morning work, while Tsering came over to breast-feed her baby while sitting beside me.

"Do you know who that man is, the one named Gehnge?" she asked.

"No, I'm not sure, but he certainly was very nice."

"He's my father," she said.

64

There goes Raymond Firth out the window, I thought. This was supposed to be a matriarchy. The father is not supposed to live with the mother's family.

"How nice, that your father gets to live with you," I volunteered.

"Yes, we are all very happy that he lives here. His family was killed during the cultural revolution. He has no family, so we let him come and stay here. He takes care of the Buddhist altar, and manages a small store in the village. He is very ill with ulcers, which he never got over after the cultural revolution."

One of the things I always bring with me is antacid for students, a remedy against the rich and often indigestible foods served at Han Chinese banquets.

"I might have some medicine that could help him," I suggested.

From that moment I became something of a medicine dispenser in the Muosuo village. Aspirin for headaches, tylenol for toothaches, antacid for stomach pains, and antibiotic ointment and bandaids for infected wounds, brought along as panacea for my ailing students, were a grand introduction for visiting Muosuo families. Great granduncle had an infected foot, an ulcer more than an inch deep, while Tsering's brother had terribly painful hemorrhoids. To this day I am still bringing medicine for Granduncle and Gehnge. Tsering's brother's case was not chronic. Preparation H and abstention from alcohol helped heal brother's affliction, along with a lengthy ceremony performed by a Buddhist monk and a Muosuo *Daba* (Dongba) priest.

The Muosuo and Nakhi Dongba rites, which I recorded with the help of Tsering and Gehnge, parallel an uncanny analogy, the ritual style of Taiwan and south China's redhead "popular" Taoists. Dongba ritual manuals are written in an ancient hieroglyphic that was used in Tibet before the coming of the modern written language, based on Buddhist Sanskrit. The hieroglyphics used by Dongba priests are found in 10th and 11th century Bon documents from Muli, Markham, and other Tibetan areas where Dongba priests still practice without Han Chinese interference.

Since Gehnge disliked the Daba rites, he hired instead a Gelugpa monk who performed a lengthy healing ritual similar to a

Taoist exorcism common to Taiwan and the coast of SE China. The Gelugpa monk fashioned twelve small demons of pestilence and one larger figure out of balls of zampa and yak (dri) butter. These were placed on a small foot-long boat, after which the monk chanted a lengthy exorcism, sprinkling incense and sorghum alcohol over the small figurines for purification and cleansing. Tsering then carried six of the figurines to the lake, casting three small statues into the lake towards the north, and three towards the west (yin). The brother carried the other six figurines out towards the hills, throwing three to the east, and three to the south (yang). The monk burned the last, larger figurine in a fire lit in the courtyard outside the entrance to the family room. I did my best to explain that a ritual was performed by Taoists in Taiwan, very similar to the Muosuo rite of healing, called "Wangyeh rite of exorcism," or "Casting out the Wangyeh boat." But Gehnge would have none of it. Only Buddhism he felt, was efficacious.

Tsering did not contradict him, but explained afterwards that women worship the mother goddess of the lake and the soil, while men worship at the Buddhist shrine. Tsering's younger brother had become a Gelugpa monk, and gone to India to study, she told me. Though the women offered sacrifice and prayers to the Buddhist shrine when Gehnge was too sick to do so, men did not do the rites reserved for women.

I asked Tsering how Gehnge got along with her mother, now that he lived with her family. Since he now was considered more like an uncle, she responded, it was alright for him to find another wife to visit. In fact he had a son by this second wife, whom he visited occasionally. The rules of matriarchy refuse to allow a man who lives within a family to have relations with a woman of the family. Her own husband, she added, could come to see her only after everyone else had gone to bed, and must leave before the others get up in the morning.

My first visit to the Muosuo was in January of 1993. It was not until January of 1997 that I at last met Tsering's husband. Though I visited the family each year for Chinese New year, and performed all of the new year rituals by the hearth and in the hills, I was never lucky enough to meet the father of her (by now) two children. The second child, a boy, had the same large eyes as his sister, and the same strong temper. But the sister was definitely the boss. She would someday be matriarch, a fact that great-grandmother, grandmother, and mother clearly prepared her for.

The last time I visited the Muosuo was January of 1997 and 1998. I went alone, without students or other foreigners to look after. It was only then that I was able to meet Tsering's husband. He came at night, after everyone else had finished dinner. When he came in, no one made a fuss or got up to greet him, except Tsering, who was obviously delighted to see him, as were the two children. She sat him by the fire, to my left. Both children rushed into his arms, and hugged him. He held them both, while he ate his dinner, obviously filled with affection and joy over seeing them.

When I got up the next morning and went to the fire to warm myself, the husband had already gone. Barr was making fried bread, and grandmother's sister, who was visiting, took grandmother's place by the fire, pouring salty tea for the early risers. Tsering soon came in, carrying the boy on her back. She sat by the fire, and then explained, as if sensing my questions without my asking.

"My husband is a Pumi, not a Muosuo," she said. "He is a truck driver, and goes for months at a time into the hills of Tibet, to ferry out the huge trees cut by the Chinese for lumber. His job is very dangerous and hard."

"He is very handsome, and filled with affection for his children," I remarked, not knowing what else to say.

"The children and I love him very much," she answered. "Maybe someday he will work closer by us."

I said no more, nor did she. Gehnge came in, and we went together to the Buddhist altar to pray. That morning, Gehnge was going to see his other family, he told me. He had to ride a horse for a day and a half to get there. I said that I would love to ride along, but Gehnge said that would be difficult. Muosuo horses were too small, and besides, the family didn't know I would be coming. Husbands go alone to visit their wives' families, bringing no one else with them.

It is now late June. I plan to go back to the Muosuo when this is finished, before returning to the States for more writing and research. The Muosuo family always wonder why I don't spend more time there.

If only I could, I answer. Maybe someday, like Joseph Rock, when my research is done, I'll live on the island in the middle of the lake, and watch the sun come up every morning.

Case 4. An Islamic Family; Xining, Qinghai

The first time that I met a member of the Xining Ma family (not their real name) was in a small hotel in Xining, on a cold September evening after a long bumpy bus ride through the back hills of Qinghai. Again with tired and hungry students in tow, we were desperately in search of dinner and a hotel. The bus driver, of Islamic Hui ethnicity, knew a fine hotel run by Hui relatives near the Xining station. I left the students in the bus, went into the hotel lobby, and was confronted with one of those situations which occur so frequently in China. Han guests who were checking out six hours after the noon time limit for leaving, were refusing in very loud voices to pay the extra half day fare. The bewildered attendants behind the desk did not know how to handle the situation.

Out from the office stepped a young woman, about twenty years of age, I guessed, with long hair combed straight to her waist, large eyes, and clear pink cheeked white complexion. Pinned to her blue uniform was a plastic ID card which said in large characters "Ma Ping, Chief Accountant, Asst. Manager." She glared at the Han officials, then spoke in a very clear and unequivocal manner.

"Excuse me, officers, this is an Islamic Hotel. According to government rules established by the *Gonganju* (PSB), we are required to charge an extra half day fee for guests who stay after the noon time check-out deadline. Since you may not have read the rules (she pointed to a sign directly behind her), I shall give you a ten percent discount." There was no more argument or other signs of discontent. The leather-coated officials paid the bill, and left.

"You were marvelous," I said, forgetting that I was waiting in line to get rooms for my students. "They were so rude. How did you stay so calm?"

"Han Chinese," she answered. "They are all that way. How may we help you this evening?"

"I have a bus load of very tired students outside. They haven't eaten yet, and need a place to stay." I did my best to be very polite.

"What kind of students are they?" she asked, in the same direct, no-nonsense manner.

"They are foreign exchange students with residence permits," I answered. "By government rules we are allowed to stay for Chinese rather than foreign prices."

"Let me see your ID papers."

I showed her my Foreign Expert card and Work Permit (*Gongzuo Zheng*). Everything was written in Chinese, with my Chinese name and title, "Professor Su Haihan."

"Su Laoshr," she said, using my professor's title, "We do not have police permission to have foreign guests here. But if you sign them in under your name and work unit, the police won't make any trouble."

So Ma Ping signed us in, two students per room, with phone, TV and shower, at Chinese rates, 60% less than larger hotels with permission to house foreigners.

"There's an Islamic restaurant in our hotel," she said. "After your students wash up and rest a bit, tell them to come down. We'll order a meal for them."

Four young Hui Islamic cooks made a superb meal for the weary students, with lots of vegetables and kosher style meat, (no pork). Ma Ping sat with them, making sure that they had enough to eat, and could order their favorite foods, such as french fried potatoes, and carmeled apples for dessert.

Each fall, for the past seven years, we have returned to Ma Ping's hotel, with the same friendly service and good prices. During that time Ma Ping's mother and father, two brothers and one younger sister, provided an excellent resource for understanding the closeness and concern of a conservative Islamic Hui Chinese family. In the words of Dru Gladney's powerful classic *Muslim Chinese*, (1991: 14)

> The Hui's defining and ordering of their world into one
> that is pure and true, turns the tables on Chinese society.
> It reverses the Durkheimian polarities of what is sacred and

69

profane in China, making the Hui *the pure* community, that rejects Chinese ritual values,...

As Gladney explains so well, the Hui term for their religious-cultural system, the *Qingzhen* or "Pure, True" faith is a powerful factor for maintaining identity:

> The different ways Hui have sought to adapt their
> ethnoreligious identity, their ideas of a pure and true
> life style, to the various Chinese sociopolitical contexts
> and to the tides of Islamic influence arriving from
> the Middle East and Central Asia have led to wide div-
> ersities of Hui identities and Islamic orders in China, as
> well as influencing the nature of their conflict and in-
> teraction with the Chinese state. (1991: 15)

Ma Ping's ancestors were immigrants from Persia. After the cruel experience of the Great Cultural Revolution, when many of the Hui were made to live with and tend pigs, and suffer other intolerable indignities, the period of recent economic expansion and growth has brought about an increase of conservative values and practices throughout Islamic China. One sees everywhere the rebuilding and high attendance at Mosques for Friday services, the wearing of the white Islamic hat as a sign of ethnic identity for men, and the veil worn by women after marriage, according to custom.

Ma Ping, as the eldest daughter of a famous Islamic doctor, trained in western and Chinese medicine, was made to learn the profession of her father from an early age. By the time she was twelve years old, Ma Ping was able to handle the basic responsibilities of a trained nurse, give injections, administer IV's, and handle the bedside care of patients in her father's large clinic.

Ma Ping wanted to be a doctor, and train as an MD in the western tradition. But since she was a daughter, not a son of her famous father, the training given her from a tender age through her nineteenth year was transferred to the elder of her younger brothers, when he was old enough to learn the trade of his father. At age nineteen Ma Ping was sent by her father to Xining, to manage a hotel for her uncle.

The uncle, like many Islamic men in China, preferred to attend the mosque and handle other business affairs, entrusting the management of the hotel to Ma Ping and other partners. Ma Ping's mother came frequently to Xining to see her daughter, sending her food and clothes from home, and bringing along the younger sister to begin training under her older sister in hotel management.

The abilities of the young Hui woman to manage more than a hotel soon became evident to the Hui business world of Xining. Projects of many kinds were brought to Ma Ping to oversee and supervise. So did marriage proposals from wealthy Han businessmen, and other professionals. A Canadian company (Overseas Chinese) tried to buy into the hotel, to increase the profit. The police asked to open a Karaoke Bar Restaurant on the 3rd floor. A wealthy doctor proposed bringing Ma Ping to the States for training in a traditional Chinese-style clinic.

All these things did not appeal to Ma Ping, or to her parents. Strict Islamic custom demands that she marry a person of Islamic faith, and bring up her children as Muslim. Ma Ping has not yet married, putting off the forming of a family until she has earned enough for an independent career, free from male domination. The pressures of her faith, and of modern society to succeed economically, in a society that values her honesty and quality-conscious service, has kept her from servitude as a housewife to a traditional Hui husband. Though custom forbids women to enter the Mosque to pray, Ma Ping follows the strict Islamic rule of bowing toward Mecca and praying daily in her own room, after her hotel work duties are finished.

Conclusion

The social and cultural customs of China's minorities are not at all similar to the majority Han. Almost no minority peoples desire or actively seek assimilation with the Han, except as a way to turn a profit in an economy that is rushing eternally forward in search of quick wealth and highly desired consumer items. The immediate goals of Han Chinese, for preferred clothes, European brand names, cars (Mercedes-Benz), high rise apartments, portable phones, and a green card for entrance to the United States (lucrative jobs), are not mirrored in the ideals or goals of the minority peoples interviewed or visited in the course of this research.

It would be wrong to suggest that all minority peoples are like the Muosuo, Aini, Tibetan nomads, or Hui whom one meets in Yunnan, Gansu, Qinghai, and Tibet proper. It would also be wrong to refuse the best aspects of modernization, such as clinics with trained doctors and valid medicine, schools with courses in native as well as foreign languages, science, and literature, and adequate roads and transportation to make the good things of modern life accessible to far away minorities.

There is also great value in making the peaceful way of life of China's minorities accessible to the worn out and jaded refugees from China's distraught and sometimes violent cities. Whatever other things are noted in telling the stories of four people from minority families, the self-evident truth in all of the above data is the overwhelming support and importance of family, in the lives of these more-or-less culturally untainted minority people.

STATISTICS, CHARTS,
AND ANALYSIS

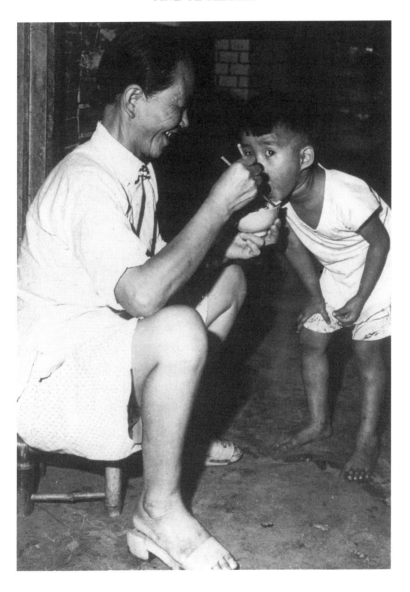

5. UNDERSTANDING THE FAMILY IN SOUTHEAST CHINA
(Wade-Giles Romanization)

There is no question of the Chineseness of Taiwan, or of its membership in the greater cultural system of mainland China, just across the straits. Like a timepiece blessedly untouched by the ravages of collectives, communes, Great Leaps and Cultural Revolutions, Taiwan has preserved a more traditional set of family and festive customs while undergoing intense economic and industrial growth. Along with the other "little dragons" of Asia (Korea, Hongkong, and Singapore), it continues to find a ready market for quality goods produced for world markets.

Unlike more crowded and physically harsh areas of Asia, Taiwan is a verdant semi-tropical island just off the coast of Fukien province in southeast China. It is blessed with a temperate climate and abundant rainfall tumbling down from high peaks towering more than 10,000 feet above sea level. The island's terraced paddy produces three crops a year and supports a population of more than 20,000,000 Chinese inhabitants. Some 240,000 Austronesian minority tribes now reside mainly in the mountains.[1]

Taiwan appears in sixth century AD Chinese historical records. Chinese settlers from southeast Fukien province just across the Taiwan Strait began arriving in great numbers towards the end of the Ming dynasty, i.e., between 1580-1644, and established a kingdom in exile opposed to the conquering Manchu-Ch'ing dynasty. Subdued towards the end of the seventeenth century, Taiwan became a province of China, and remains today, both culturally and ethnically, a part of the Chinese nation.

Most of the Chinese from southeast Fukien who moved to Taiwan during the Ming and Ch'ing dynasties (settlers continued to come to Taiwan throughout the Ch'ing dynasty, up until the Japanese invasion in 1895) spoke the southern Fukien (Min) dialect common to Hsiamen, Chang-chou, Ch'üan-chou, and other areas across the Taiwan Strait. Speakers of the Hakka language from west Fukien and north Kwangtung province also moved to Taiwan during this period, but never in the large numbers of the dominant southern Fukien settlers.

By the end of the Ch'ing dynasty Taiwan became the most prosperous province of China, with the first railroad, thriving tea, sugar, and lumber industries, and an abundance of vegetables, fruit, and rice. Two crops of rice a year, and one of vegetables, was produced by Taiwan's industrious farmers.

The wealthy families of Taiwan's newly affluent frontier society soon established schools of Confucian learning, and in 1823 produced the first doctor of letters, from the prosperous Cheng clan of Hsinchu city. Taoists from Fukien and far away places such as Mao Shan in Chiangsu, Buddhists from the Ch'an (Zen) schools of southeast China, and scholars of the Confucian tradition came to serve the needs of the expanding Chinese cultural economy. Were it not for political changes beyond the control of the struggling pioneer families, Taiwan's wealth could have been a contributing factor to the growth of modern China.

Named Isla Formosa (Beautiful Island) by the Portuguese and Spanish in the late sixteenth century, Taiwan was host first to contingents of Spanish, then to Dutch trading missions. Rising Japanese military and economic interests, thwarted from plans to annex more than Hsiamen city in the 1880's,[2] invaded and set up a colonial government in Taiwan in 1895, making it a part of the expanding Japanese empire.

Dismayed by the inability of the Chinese government to come to its rescue, and the cruelty of the Japanese colonial invaders, who attempted to alter the Chinese cultural system to fit a Japanese-style legal structure, the populace of Taiwan held tightly to the single most powerful means at hand for survival, the observation of household and temple ritual. Family festival and customary law became powerful weapons for personal integrity and cultural preservation.

At first the Japanese attempted to enforce the practice of the Japanese legal system on the Chinese of Taiwan. This attempt ended in total failure. A special law was promulgated in 1906, replacing the Japanese legal system, and declaring Taiwan-Chinese religious and social customs as a special kind of private and customary law.[3] The promulgation of this law coincided with the establishment of the Household Registration system (Chin: *hu-chi*; Jpn: *koseki*). The effect of the new law was to give legal status to the family customs of birth, adoption, marriage, and burial. Perhaps for the first time in its history, the Japanese colonialist legal system yielded to private customary law and ritual for the Chinese families of Taiwan. Judgements made by the Japanese high courts in Taipei and elsewhere in Taiwan were based on Chinese customary practice. When the Colonial Government of Taiwan published the final code of civil and commercial law in 1922, the Chinese rules of family relationships and succession were given the status of exceptions to ordinary Japanese law.

The Japanese attempted to codify the customs, including marriage and adoption, used by the Chinese families of Taiwan, in order to regulate the household registration system. Terms used by the Chinese to describe a boy or girl adopted into the family, the types of marriage, and other relationships were used as titles for entries in the official household registration forms kept in the city bureau of public records. The registration forms, begun in 1906, were similar to those kept by the household registration bureau in Japan, but were more detailed in order to maintain colonial police rule over the population of Taiwan. For the most part, Chinese rather than Japanese terminology, was used to register family members.

More than twenty-seven entries were made for each member of the family. Data included date and place of birth, parentage, order of sibling rank (first, second, third brother, sister, etc.), ethnolinguistic origin (Fukien, Hakka, mainland Chinese, Korean, Japanese, etc.), occupation of household head, political reliability, vaccinations and inoculations, kind and date of marriage or adoption, division of household, divorce, physical defects, encounters with the police, movement in and out of the household, bound feet, and so forth. Other details were appended to the record of each individual by the watchful Japanese police. When the head of a household died, the family register was bound into a separate volume, and a new household register begun dating from the selection of a new household head.

The household registers, bound year-by-year and stored in the city archives, became a marvelous source of statistical data for studying the Chinese family. When the Japanese left the island at the end of World War II, the decision was made to preserve the registers as a legal aid to solving inheritance, descent, consanguinal and affinal relationship problems. The household registration system was continued by the Chinese government in a more benign and humanistic form until the present day. The household registers serve as a reference for employment, vital statistics, (birth, adoption, marriage, and death figures), military service, certificates of identification, and so forth.

Concerning the household registration system initiated by the Japanese in 1906, it became crucial for the civil servants who made entries in the city records to understand the significance of the terms used by the Chinese. The legal expert and high circuit judge Aneba Shohei explained the differences in the Japanese and Chinese systems in his definitive study published in 1934.[4] Relationships in the Chinese family system are generated by birth, marriage, and adoption, a classification which at face value seemed the same as civil law in Japan. The Chinese concept of "relative": (Jpn: *shinseki*; Chin: *ch'in-ch'i*) however, was much wider than the Japanese legal term allowed. "Relative" to the Chinese way of thinking included a *chieh* concubine, a *simpua* girl brought into the family as a child to marry a son of the family when older, and other terms unfamiliar to the Japanese. Four distinct kinds of relationships were defined for entry in the household registers:

1. Natural relatives, i.e., lineal and collateral relatives.

2. Spouses, including major (consenting adults), minor (with a child bride on maturity), uxorilocal (Jpn. *muko-yoshi*, Chin: *Chao-hsü*), and concubine marriages.

3. Affinal relatives, by marriage from major and minor (*simpua*) ties.

4. Quasi-relatives, i.e., step-parents and step-children, foster parents and foster children, adopted children, illegitimate children, relations between a concubine and the husband's first wife and parents.

A husband-concubine marriage was defined as a man with a first wife who marries another woman (women) for the purpose of producing descendants, with or without permission of his first wife. A concubine marriage leads to a quasi-relationship between the husband's first wife and parents, as in category #4 above, with the concubine and her children. Children resulting from the union between husband and concubine-wife have the right to share the inheritance with other members of the clan, and even become heirs to the household headship, on occasion.

The Taiwanese/Minnan term *simpua* (called *t'ung-yang hsi* in mandarin), refers to a young girl brought into a family for the purpose of later marrying a natural or adopted son. Even though the *simpua* girl is not given the family name, since Chinese law demands that marriage be surname exogamous, (i.e., people with the same surname may not marry) the effects of bringing in a *simpua* girl are analogous to adoption. The term therefore means adopting a bride-to-be into the family at an early age. Adoption of a *simpua* may take place soon after birth, and occurs frequently in some Taiwan areas up to age ten. There are two forms of *simpua* adoptions: 1) in a family which has a boy to be the *simpua*'s future husband; 2) a family in which there is no boy at the time of adoption. In the former case, adoption generates the legal status of quasi-spouse, and consequently the relationship of affine between both sides of the adopting families. In the latter case affinal relationships with the girl's family begin with the birth or adoption of a boy in the adopting family. I.e., the girl adopted as a *simpua* into a family with no son is considered to be an affine of the adopting family, but the *simpua*'s family is not related affinally until a son is born.

These considerations are important because of the relationship of kinship to attendance at the rites of passage. According to universal Chinese custom, kinship is computed in the following fashion:

1. Blood relatives up to the sixth degree (consanguine).
2. Spouse.
3. Quasi-spouse, i.e., husband-to-concubine, son-to-*simpua*.
4. Affinal relatives (by marriage) to the third degree.

The husband-concubine marriage generates relationships only with the legitimate wife and the husband's parents. These relationships are considered to be extremely important in the case of funeral ritual, determining who is to be present at various functions and specific segments of the ritual.

It was not until the law of 1922 was promulgated that the above categories became defined in clear legal terms, a result of the inadequacy of Japanese law with regard to Chinese familial rela-

79

tionships. The deficiencies were most pronounced in the concubine and *simpua* form of marriage, and legal precedent needed to be established in accord with the categories used in the household registration forms.

Since the quasi-spouse was not considered to be a legitimate wife in the Japanese system, in civil and criminal cases bigamy and adultery could not always be handled as legal cases in court. In a series of legal decisions, the Japanese soon defined the customary legal status of the concubine's quasi-marriage, as reflected in the household registers.

In the Chinese customary system, recognition of paternity constituted a concubine relationship. Yet, if a concubine decided to marry another man as a legitimate wife, divorce proceedings were unnecessary and the concubine could not be accused of adultery or bigamy.[5]

Among other concepts of the Chinese family unfamiliar to the Japanese legal system was the institution of household head, *hu-chu* (Jpn: *koshu*). In the Japanese system, where primogeniture is the determining factor in deciding succession to the household headship, the oldest son of the family was automatically made household head. In Chinese custom, however, the so called family head, *Chia-chang* was chosen on the basis of being the person most capable of handling the family's affairs. The position of family head usually belonged to the oldest person most capable or most powerful in transacting family business. This position did not always correspond to the oldest legitimate son, or even to a male member of the family. The household registers often list a second son, adopted son, concubine's son, a *simpua*, an illegitimate child, or a favored daughter as succeeding to the household headship.

The household registers list eight categories of women who become household heads, constituting, as mentioned above, about 11-12% of the city household registrations:

1. Widows.
2. Courtesans (*Geisha*, in the Japanese system).
3. Single girls working in the city.
4. Daughters of rich merchants with an uxorilocal husband (*chao-hsü*).

5. Widows with an uxorilocal husband (*chao-fu*).

6. Prostitutes living together in a private (non-business) household.

7. Wives with husbands away on business or in military service.

8. Concubines living in a house separate from the legitimate wife.

A supplement to the special law of 1906 instituting the household registration system, determined in 1907 that the Chinese word *chia-chang* for family head coincided in legal usage with the Japanese term *ko-shu* household head (Chin: *hu-chu*). The person called *chia-chang* in Chinese was to be listed as *hu-chu* in the household registers.

In Japanese civil law, all members of the family call themselves by the family surname, but in the Chinese custom there are many family members who are not allowed or do not wish to do so. Thus the *simpua* girls adopted in to be a bride of a son of the family must by the surname exogamy rule of the Chinese system keep their maiden surname. Likewise the concubine, slave-maid (Taiwanese: *ca-bo-kan*), a husband of a widow married for the second time (*chao-fu*) and the husband of a girl marrying uxorilocally (*chao-hsü*), all keep their own surname when entering into the Chinese family, and therefore are listed in the household register with their own family names.

Some of the Chinese customs were however altered by the Japanese registration system. One of these changes occurred in the manner of signing the wife's surname. Wives and concubines always sign themselves by their own surname in the Chinese system, due to the prohibition of marriage between people of the same family name. Between 1906 and 1922 the wife's maiden name was entered in the household register, followed by the character *shih*, as a convenient way for the city registrar to indicate a woman. Following the promulgation of the civil code on January 1, 1922, the woman's husband's surname was entered first in the register, followed by her own surname, and the character *shih*. After the promulgation of the 1922 law, women began to sign legal documents with their maiden name and the character *shih* in order to conform to the Japanese legal system.

Other departures from Japanese civil law, requiring adjustments in the household registers were the practices of dividing the household, and retirement of the household head. In the first instance, there were two ways of dividing the Chinese household, i.e., breaking away from the ancestral home and founding a new family (Chin: *fen-chia*; Jpn: *bunkei*). The first, called (Chin:) *I-ts'ai pieh-chü*, referred to a newly founded family with no right to inheri tance, while the second, *T'ung-ts'ai pieh-chü* referred to a divided household with the right of inheritance. In the Japanese system the latter was not really a divided household, since the entire inheritance was given only to the eldest son. But both cases were nevertheless given the term "divided household" (*fen-chia*) in the registers.

Likewise, there was no equivalent system in the Japanese civil code to account for the retirement of a household head, a practice important to the Chinese family system. The Chinese term *yin-chü* (Jpn: *inkyo*) for recluse was used to refer to the head of a Chinese family who retired and divided his property amongst his heirs, in order to avoid dispute after death, and to retire from direct control over the family business. In the Japanese legal system such a division was called a donation rather than inheritance, but the Japanese legal term *inkyo* was used in the registers, and adapted into Taiwanese language to indicate the household head who divided his property before death and retired from the legal status of household head.

As stated above, the Chinese legal system recognized four kinds of marriage to establish the family, i.e., major, minor, uxorilocal, and concubine. Major marriage is almost the same in the traditional Chinese sense as in western and Japanese legal terms, except that in traditional Chinese usage, it need not be recorded in a public records office. Certification by a legal witness, called *chu-hun jen*, was sufficient for a valid marriage in the traditional Chinese legal system.[6] The Japanese colony and modern China require registration. Studies in the People's Republic of China show that the *Chu-hun jen* is still considered more important than official registration.

It was also the custom throughout most of China to pay a price for the bride. Both sides are required to give and receive gifts, and the bride must bring a dowry to her groom's family as a part of the

82

wedding contract. The acceptance of the bride price by the girl's family however, does not affect the validity of the marriage itself. A marriage could be called off after receiving a price for the bride. The person who accepts the money is usually the lineal ascendant of the bride, but could be the bride herself. Likewise, the person paying the price for the bride is usually the groom's lineal ascendant, but sometimes the groom pays the money himself. In Hsinchu city (northwest Taiwan) the bride price is always counted and sent back to the groom's family, leading to a common saying in Taiwan, "Marry a girl from Hsinchu, but give a daughter in marriage anywhere else." The custom of sending back the bride price is found in many areas of China, especially in environments with highly developed merchant and educational systems.[7]

The husband-concubine marriage had the same legal effect for the children of the concubine union as a major marriage, but the ceremony was extremely simple and almost without public notice. After the establishment of the new legal system in 1906, and especially after the promulgation of the legal code of 1922, it became easy for the concubine to appeal for divorce in the courts, without finding a legal husband to marry in the major fashion. Though the Japanese expressed disapproval of the concubine system, it was not until the post-war period and the establishment of anti-bigamy laws that the concubine marriage became an anachronism in Taiwan. Many cases of concubine marriages are recorded until the end of the war in 1945.

Two kinds of uxorilocal marriages are recorded in the household registers, the *chao-fu*, and the *chao-hsü*, as stated above. A *chao-fu* indicates an uxorilocal marriage in the case where a widow becomes household head after her first husband's death, and then marries in a husband to be her consort. A document is drawn up in a standard contract form, agreeing beforehand how many children resulting from the relationship will be given the wife's or the *chao-fu* husband's surname.

A *chao-hsü* refers to an arrangement where the daughter of a family calls in a husband who is registered as a member of her family. As in the *chao-fu* case, a contractual agreement is reached determining how many children resulting from the union will be given the surname of the wife's family, or the name of the father.

Four reasons are given in notes appended to the registers, and in sociological literature on Taiwan, for the occurrence of the uxorilocal marriage:

1. The head of the family is too old to support the household, and an older daughter is provided with a *chao-hsü* to help the family business.

2. A family needs a legal heir as household head, and lacking sons, prefers to marry a daughter or *simpua* in the uxorilocal fashion, rather than adopt a son.

3. The family desires to have as many workers as possible.

4. The family does not want their daughter to be married out, due to love or deep-felt need for her.

The difference in the uxorilocal marriage in Japan and China is that in the Japanese system the boy takes the surname of the wife's family, i.e., he is legally adopted as a member of the wife's family by marriage, and all children are given the wife's surname.

By Chinese custom, however, the uxorilocally married husband, i.e., the *chao-hsü* and the *chao-fu* keep their own family name, and do not become an adopted son of the wife's parents. Not only does the uxorilocal husband keep his own surname, but he also may arrange by contract that some of the children born by the union are given his surname, in order to continue his family line. In the household registers, children given the surname of the uxorilocal husband are listed as lodgers, not as children of the wife's family. Chapter 2 shows examples of such contractual arrangements.

Two other terms, used interchangeably with *chao-fu* occur in the household registers, i.e., *ju-fu* and *chao-ju*. In the first mentioned *ju-fu* case, the wife is already the household head. It does not always follow that the wife of a *chao-fu* is head of the family, or that she will continue to be head after the marriage. All possible combinations and variations are found in the registers. It seems to be most common that the oldest child of an uxorilocal marriage takes the wife's surname, and the other children the husband's. But there are some cases where all of the children take the husband's surname, and other cases where the husband moves back to his original family with his wife, leaving behind one son with the wife's family's surname. Such a case is called *ch'u-she* in the registers, after which the marriage is legally treated as a major marriage, with the wife declaring independence from her parental household. There are two causes listed for such a change of uxorilocal residence: 1) At the time of engagement, both sides agree to an eventual change. 2) After the marriage, following a discussion and mutual agreement by both sides, a change of status occurs.

Parental authority legally belongs to the mother of the children given her surname, or to the father if the children are given his name. In the case of the death of the mother, the children owe obedience to their father, regardless of name.

Minor marriage, as defined above, is a term used for marriage with a *simpua* or *yang-hsi* adopted child bride-to-be, and a son of the family. The legal conditions for establishing the *simpua* form of adoption are the following: 1) The surname of the girl is differs from the adopting family; 2) The family agree contractually to take her as bride of their son, though the son need not yet be born or adopted into the family; 3) The girl is legally adopted into the husband-to-be family, who assume the duty to provide her with a husband, and treat her as an affine.

The *simpua* is not an adopted daughter, and so does not have a foster-parent relationship with the family that adopts her. Rather, she has affinal relationships with the family, and her husband-to-be is considered to have affinal relationships (as by marriage) with her original family.

Though the *simpua* is in some way contractually obligated to marry a son of the adopting family, no one could force her to do so, should she be unwilling to marry in the adopting family. Cases of cancellation of the *simpua* contract and return to the girl's original family (*li-yüan*) occur frequently in the registers. Furthermore the Japanese special law of Taiwan gave the *simpua* the right to appeal the cancellation of adoptive relationships should the designated boy decide to marry another girl.[8] The registers show great variation in the percentage of *simpua* who actually marry into the adopting family. The percentage is much higher for rural farming families than for the urban gentry-scholars and merchants. In the Hsinchu city registers, as will be seen in the following chapters, there is hardly a family without a *simpua*, less of 10% of which actually marry into the family which adopts them.

There are two major classifications of parent-child relationships in the household registers, namely: 1) natural relations, and 2) relations by adoption. Natural relations are classified as follows:

1. legitimate children
2. children of a concubine
3. illegitimate children

The legal difference between an illegitimate child (*szu-sheng-tzu*) and the child of a concubine (*shu-tzu*) in the household registers, is that the natural father's name of the concubine's child is listed in the register. Public recognition by the father in the form of household registration legally initiated the concubine relationship in the Chinese family, a distinction that does not exist in Japanese law.

If the categories of natural children did not require too much adaptation of the Japanese legal system to Chinese custom, the categories of adopted children, on the other hand were entirely different from Japan. Three kinds of adoption were commonly practiced by the Chinese families of Taiwan:

1. The *kuo-fang-tzu* (also, *kuo-chi-tzu*) a boy adopted from a branch of the family with the same surname, often to be head of the adopting family. Ties within the family remain unchanged.

2. The *ming-ling-tzu* boy adopted from a clan with different surname.[9] This relationship, also described in Taiwanese as *mai-duan*, referred to a boy who had been purchased, and therefore cut off all relationships with the original family. The custom, discouraged by the Japanese, was nevertheless widely practiced in Taiwan

3. The *yang-nü* girl, adopted into the family to be daughter of the household. Unlike the *simpua*, the *yang-nü* girls could take the same surname and were legally members of the adopting family.

In all three of the above cases, the status of the adopted child was considered to be the same as a legitimate child, but in fact the ming-ling-tzu boy had the legal right to only a half share of the inheritance, and so was called a "half son." The *yang-nü* adopted daughter was often nothing more than a servant, as were the *simpua*.

The reason for the adoption of such a high rate of seeming *yang-nü* and *simpua* girls as servants seems to have been due to two factors: 1) the negative attitude of the colonial Japanese government to the purchase of *ca-po-kan* slave girls; 2) the higher esteem and social status of the *simpua* form of adoption. The family adopting a *simpua* girl was legally bound to see to her marriage, a deciding factor certainly with the family giving away or selling one of their daughters.[10]

Finally, there are many cases of adoption in certain areas of Taiwan done with the clear purpose of forcing the adopted girl into a career of prostitution.[11] These girls are known euphemistically as "filial daughters," because their earnings are used to support the adopting families. Such *simpua* and *yang-nü* help adoptive brothers and sisters through college, or support impoverished adoptive parents.

The city of Chia-i in central Taiwan and the area of Hai-shan and Shu-lin in the Taipei basin are noted for supplying many such *simpua* to the barbershop front houses, bars, and tea shops of the larger industrial areas of Taiwan. The status of these girls was considered to be higher than the slave girl or servant. There are many cases in the urban household registers of courtesans and other *simpua* professionals who eventually found their own family by adopting children and supporting a large foster family.

The practice of adopting a girl to be a bride of a future son of the family was so widespread that the Japanese courts and records officials were hard put to find a single cause for the custom. Six circumstances preceding *simpua* adoption are found in the urban and rural household registers, as recorded in the works of Aneba, Suzuki, and the other studies of colonial period Taiwanese society. These reasons are not exhaustive, but cover the majority of cases found in the Hsinchu city registers analyzed in chapter 6.

First, many informants of the rural agricultural countryside told the Japanese that the *simpua* minor marriage was less expensive for the bride's and the groom's side of the family, and therefore popular in poor areas. The exorbitant cost of a major marriage is hard to recover. A simple contract or at most a small token gift to the girl's family suffice to pay for a *simpua* bride. Furthermore, the price of raising and educating a girl, only to have her married out to another family, could be saved by the *simpua* adoption at an early age. The household registers of Hsinchu city show, however, that *simpua* adoptions also occur in middle and upper class families, though not as frequently as in farming areas.

Second, it is said that the mother-in-law and daughter-in-law relationship is much smoother with the *simpua* minor marriage than with a major marriage bride. The *simpua* who has been brought up by her future mother-in-law, is less of a stranger than an adult bride brought into the family through major marriage. The urban household registers give examples of *simpua* girls elevated to the household headship, and provided with an uxorilocal husband, even with consanguinal children present in the family.

Third, some informants claim that a family who wanted to find a maid servant or some sort of help for the women of the household, did so by bringing in a girl from a poorer family, and registering her as a *simpua* child bride with the Japanese *Koseki* registration office, simply because this was the simplest way to cut through the red tape and bureaucratic procedures imposed by the benighted Japanese colonial government. The term *simpua* was taken in the literal sense by the registration office, i.e., the adopting family supposedly took care of arranging a marriage for the girl brought in as a *simpua*, but had no such obligations for the *yangnü* adopted daughter.

Fourth, newlyweds who had no children or families without a daughter, are highly like to adopt a *simpua* girl even before a first child is born, a fact proven in many rural and urban family registers. A popular proverb is quoted, "Adopt a *simpua* and heaven will send a boy baby." In fact there is no proof in the registers that adopting a *simpua* had any effect on fertility of the newly wed mother. Rather, the pressure on the young wife to cook, clean, and do washing is greatly alleviated by adopting a *simpua* immediately after marriage, to help with the household chores. In such a case, the *simpua* is little more than an unpaid servant.

Fifth, when the foster parents are ill, or have no children, a *simpua* is frequently adopted to look after them. A *simpua* can then be married in the uxorilocal manner, as a safe way to preserve the family name and fortune. Hsinchu statistics show that single parents are less likely to adopt a *ming-ling-tzu* boy, who might return to his parents, than bring up a *simpua* girl to manage the family fortunes.

Sixth, a special case occurs in some households where the parents die, leaving behind a boy who is very young. In this case, an older *simpua* is adopted to fulfill the obligation of burning incense before the ancestor shrine, for the first three years after death, as required by customary ritual law in traditional China.

Whichever form of registration was chosen, it is clear from the analysis of the Hsinchu City registers that there was very little distinction made in the reality of everyday life between an adopted daughter and a *simpua* child bride, from the evidence found in the Hsinchu city statistics.

In spite of the reasons given by informants for adopting a *simpua*, there is no solid evidence in the *koseki* household registers that adopting a *simpua* had any effect on fertility, keeping the household from dividing, or noticeable differences with the status of a *yang-nü* adopted girl or a *ca-bo-gan* slave girl. Other than the slightly higher legal status afforded a *simpua* in the Japanese colonial registration office, (i.e., the adopting family provides for her marriage), the *simpua* was in fact little different from a slave girl.

The Japanese sociologist Okada Jun reports in his 1949 survey, that there were four alleged reasons given by his informants for preferring a *simpua* adoption:[12] 1) A family with too many girls tries to build social relations with a family that needs more girls. 2) In the case of a widow, a single woman, or a woman with an illegitimate child, children could be cared for until marriageable age by the *simpua* adoptee. 3) Some give their daughters away due to a superstitious belief, i.e., born on an unlucky day or year. 4) Poor families cannot support more children. Okada also noticed that in the city of Hsiamen, (then called Amoy) across the straits from Taiwan, there were no *simpua* adoptions due to an oversupply of girls and a dirth of young men, who had gone off to the diaspora of Southeast Asia to seek employment.

In summary, the registers used in our study cover for the most part urban families of Hsinchu city, during the period from 1870, when the average household head surveyed in the first registration of 1906 was born, until 1972, when the microfilming and study of the registers was begun. The registers analyzed in the following chapter show that the most important single element in the social, economic, and ritual life of Hsinchu was and continues to be the family. No matter what form the *Jiating* family household takes, its centrality in the daily life of the individual is inescapable and irreplaceable.

———

Notes

1. Nine ethnic groups of Austronesian linguistic and cultural origin inhabit the hills (and at one time the plains) of Taiwan. Similar to Mainland China, where an official policy makes efforts to preserve language and culture, the aboriginal peoples of China are gradually sinicized (made Chinese) through public education and economic progress.

2. Japan's occupation of the port of Hsiamen, defeat of the Russian navy, and occupation of Taiwan at the turn of the 19th century were signs of coming military, and more recently, economic designs to power and domination in Asia.

3. See Aneba Shohei, *Taiwan Tokushu Horitsu no Kenkyu (A Study of the Special Laws of Taiwan),* Taipei: 1934, p. 206

4. Op. Cit., note 3.

5. Op. Cit., Taiwan Supreme Court, 1905, 1917.

6. For the role of the *chu-hun jen* in the overall wedding ritual, see M. Saso, *Blue Dragon White Tiger*, ch. 4.

7. Hsinchu seems to have been the only place in Taiwan to send back the bridal money. Many areas of Fukien, and Kwangtung Province, however, also follow this practice. Informants in Honolulu say that the areas of Chung-shan, Siyap, and Lungdu (from whence the majority of Chinese in Honolulu come) followed this practice.

8. See Aneba, p. 263, #3.

9. The term *ming-ling-tzu*, taken from the *Shih Ching (Book of Odes)* is derived from the name of a moth which lays its eggs in the nest of a wasp, to be nourished with the wasp larvae until mature.

10. It is hard to give a single reason for the popularity of *simpua* adoptions in some parts of China, and total absence of this phenomenon in other areas. See the "six reasons" alleged by the Japanese courts, immediately below.

11. Wolf, Margery, 1972: pp. 205-214.

12. Okada, Jun (Uzuru), *Kiso Shakai (The Basic Structure of Chinese Society)*, Taipei: 1949, p. 55.

6. MARRIAGE AND THE FAMILY IN HSINCHU CITY
(Wade-Giles Romanization)

The old town of Hsinchu, called *Tek-ts'am*, was a walled, small, traditional city with a population of 8,523 in 1841. (see *Taiwan Sheng, Hsinchu Hsien-chih Kao*, Vol. 4, *Jen-min Chih*, Hsinchu: Wen-Hsien Wei-yüan Hui, 1957, p. 35). The majority of the town dwellers came from Ch'uan-chou, the port town well known as the home of wealthy traders in Fukien province. Even after Hsinchu's wall was torn down by the Japanese, the town remained almost solidly Fukienese. A survey conducted by the Japanese in 1928 shows that less than 10% of the city dwellers were Hakka. (Ibid., p. 41). Chapter 5 examines marriages in this traditional city of north Taiwan, based on the household registers (Jpn: *koseki*; Ch: *hu-chi*) maintained in the city bureau of vital statistics.

Hsinchu had two prominent nineteenth century clans. One was wealthy from the salt monopoly franchise, and the other produced the first *chin-shih* degree of Taiwan in 1823. (*Hsinchu Ts'ung-chih*, Hsinchu: Wen-Hsien Wei-yüan Hui, 1952, p. 140). When the first family built a glittering villa inside the wall, near the west gate, the second did the same just outside of the north gate. Both villas served as cultural centers for Hsinchu, open to the wealthy, that is, the absentee landlords and city officials, and the educated (or caterers to the wealthy and educated). The invitees to the numerous parties and poetry readings held at the villas were the major components of Hsinchu's high society. Their descendants maintained a position of eminence through the fifty years of Japanese occupation, into the modern day.

Due to this tradition, our *koseki* records contain a large number of absentee landlords, as well as the typical artisans and merchants of the average Chinese city. The areas of the city analyzed in our study are Northgate and Westgate in the old township. To these city districts we added statistics from the districts of Shui-t'ien, Lun-tzu, K'o-ya, immediately to the north and the west of the city, respectively, where farming was the main occupation. These areas were chosen because the population remained fairly stable throughout the time period studied. Other parts of the city, such as the Eastgate district which was occupied by the Japanese colonial government from 1895-1945, and Southgate where migrant laborers, markets, and hostels were numerous, did not provide pertinent information concerning the Chinese family. Though interesting for other reasons, we did not include these areas in our survey.

We first classified the sampling population by year of birth, then categorized individuals as: 1) born in the districts, (designated as "O" for original, or blood-related family in our records); 2) "A" for adopted in, and newcomers to the city. Newcomers in this case are those who moved their permanent address, mainly from Hsinchu county, into the township. Those who were under the age of ten at the time of migration were not counted as newcomers, since they were raised and educated in the same way the city children, thereby accepted as city folk by the time of marriage.

A. Statistical Report of Marriage in Hsinchu

To show the composition of the population sampling, we constructed Table 1. The classifications are: 1) outsiders (i.e., those who had permanent addresses elsewhere, such as temporary lodgers or employees of the resident); 2) born in; 3) entered by adoption; 4) entered by marriage; 5) entered by migration.

Table 1. *Composition of population sampled. Number of married males who entered the districts by:*

	outsider	born in	adoption	marriage	migration
1891-1895	4	178	13	23	30
1896-1900	11	220	33	22	48
1901-1905	3	272	31	20	55
1906-1910	9	370	65	17	78
1911-1915	8	395	59	10	61
1916-1920	11	397	42	7	65

From the above figures we can see that the majority of our sample population was born and raised in the north and westgate districts of Hsinchu city. All of the household registers from which the samples were taken could be traced from their origins, i.e., prior to 1896, through 1945 and into the modern period. Since The proportion of "born in" to "moved in" did not change significantly by increasing the number of people sampled, we can take the above figures to be typical of males who married in north and west Hsinchu.

In Table 2, we traced all the males born in the district to marriageable age. The category "untraceable" was used to indicate those who went out of our sampling by moving elsewhere, or because of the drastic district change imposed by the Japanese colonial government. Premature death and adoption out will be discussed separately.

Table 2. *Birth, premature death, adoption out (A.O.), and marriage age reached by males born in the district*

	died before:		A.O. before:		untraceable	reached	total
	15	25	15	25			
1891-1895	*	6	2	1	23	146	178
1896-1900	*	4	5*	1	30	175	222
1901-1905	18*	3	5*	1	49	195	271
1906-1910	84	9	18	4	44	209	368
1911-1915	9	10	28	5	55	227	394
1916-1920	68	10	21	2	120	176	397

N.B. * means that the records are incomplete.

Table 3 shows the forms of marriage entered upon by males born in the city, and tests whether the forms of marriage changed as time progressed towards the present. Amongst the males born in Hsinchu, the "standard" form (Major, M) was always dominant.

Though the percentage of males who were married in the minor (m) or uxorilocal (Ux) (n.b., uxorilocal means here males married out in the uxorilocal fashion) declined steadily, the changes over the thirty-year period were not significantly large. This, of course, was because neither the minor nor the uxorilocal form of marriage was ever dominant amongst males born in the studied area at any given period within thirty-five years. The statistics summarized here demonstrate that marriage forms remained relatively constant in the urban family.

Table 3. *Percentage of marriage patterns of males born in Hsinchu*

	M	m	Ux & Single	Total for period
1891-	112	9	23	144 (12.9%)
1895	77.8%	6.2%	16.0%	
1896-	123	23	28	174 (15.5%)
1900	70.7%	13.2%	16.1%	
1901-	139	22	32	193 (17.2%)
1905	72.%	11.4%	16.6%	
1906-	155	22	31	208 (18.6%)
1910	74.5%	10.6%	14.9%	
1911-	173	14	38	225 (20.2%)
1915	76.9%	6.2%	16.9%	
1916-	123	12	40	175 (15.6%)
1920	70.3%	6.9%	22.8%	(100%)

Note that the marriages entered into by males born during this period actually occurred, for the most part, between 1910 and 1945, and represent statistics derived from families currently functioning in Hsinchu city. Single males and uxorilocal males are counted together in the third column, since neither are listed as heads of families in the registers, and the pool from which uxorilocal males are drawn is taken from the third category, as shown in Table 5.

We also note that there were no significant changes in marriage form over the period from 1880 to 1945. Though minor marriage has become almost non-existent in the modern period, uxorilocal marriage can still be found in urban and farming districts.

B. Marriage, Occupation, and Socio-economic Status

Since the time element did not make any significant difference in the marriage forms in Hsinchu, the next question to ask is whether or not any other element than time had a correlation with the form of marriage. In order to test such a possible variation, we divided the population into five classes, according to socio-economic status listed in the household registers, and records in the tax office. The five classes are: 1) wealthy landlords; 2a) wealthy merchants; 2b) middle class merchants and artisans; 2c) poor merchants, artisans, farmers; and 3) coolie or laborers. The criteria for the division are listed in the appendix to chapter 5. From an analysis of these statistics we can see that the socio-economic status did change during the Japanese period, with a shift towards the middle and away from either extreme, i.e., away from the extremely rich and the very poor.

Table 4. *Changes in population distribution according to five grades of socio-economic status, marriages contracted from 1891-1945*

	1	2a	2b	2c	3	totals
1891-	31	42	36	30	37	176
1895	17.5%	23.9%	20.5%	17.0%	21.0%	(10%)
1896-	52	43	43	30	44	212
1900	24.5%	20.3%	20.3%	14.2%	20.7%	(12.0%)
1901-	64	63	41	40	57	265
1905	24.2%	23.7%	15.5%	15.1%	21.5%	(15.1%)
1906-	57	71	80	81	68	357
1910	16.0%	19.9%	22.4%	22.7%	19.0%	(20.3%)
1911-	56	89	81	72	74	372
1915	15.1%	23.9%	21.8%	19.3%	19.9%	(21.1%)
1916-	54	93	90	66	75	378
1920	14.3%	24.6%	23.8%	17.5%	19.8%	(21.5%)
total:	314	401	371	319	355	1,760

$X2 = 32.56$ X2o (5% level) = 31.4

The null hypothesis that socio-economic status did not change chronologically is rejected on the 5% level. The Chi square test against Table 4 shows that there was a slight shift over the tested period towards the middle-middle (2b) class.

Table 5 was then compiled, to see if there were significant differences in marriage forms amongst the five socio-economic statuses. Here we see that Grade 1 and Grade 2a have more than 80% of their male offspring marrying in the standard form. While the percentage of major marriages in the two upper grades remained high, we can see that the marriage forms did vary significantly for the three lower categories. But the table must be altered slightly in the case of the uxorilocal marriage, for the good reason that there might have been more migrant males who married out in the uxorilocal fashion before migration, which records do not show in the city registers. That is, some of the records are incomplete in the city, showing only those who actually moved into the district. It is obvious, nevertheless, that the well born males had a much smaller proportion of the minor form of marriage than farmers, artisans, or coolies.

Table 5. *Socio-economic Status and Marriage Form, 1891-1945*

class	Major	minor	Uxor/S.	Total
1	153	8	23	184
	83.2%	4.3%	12.5%	(17.3%)
2a	243	13	33	289
	84.1%	5%	11.4%	(27.1%)
2b	146	24	32	202
	72.3%	11.9%	15.8%	(19.0%)
2c	128	24	36	188
	68.1%	12.8%	19.1%	(17.7%)
3	126	22	54	202
	62.4%	10.9%	26.7%	(19.0%)
Total	796	91	178	1,065

A further analysis shows a difference of marriage forms, for males born in the family, ("O" category), adopted in, or migrated into Hsinchu ("A" category). Adopted sons and migrants were far more likely to be married in the minor or uxorilocal manner than were sons born into the family. In Table 6 we compare the marriage forms of the three categories of males, that is, males born in the city, adopted into the districts, and migrating into the district. Our findings show that economic status was the deciding factor. Note that the uxorilocal category was computed from the birth cohort of females born between 1891-1920, to test the rate of uxorilocal marriages in Hsinchu city.

Table 6. *Types of male marriage between 1891-1945*

	Major	Minor	Ux or S	Total
born	790	101	192	1083
	72.9%	9.3%	17.7%	(72.1%)
A.I.	119	39	24	182
	65.4%	21.4%	13.2%	(12.1%)
migrant	167	44	26	237
	70.5%	8.5%	11.0%	(15.8%)
Totals	1076	184	242	1502
	71.6%	12.3%	16.1%	(100%)

$X2 = 36.68$ $X2o$ (0.5% level) $= 14.86$

The null hypothesis that the difference in 3 categories has no relation to marriage pattern is rejected on the 0.5% level.

Table 7. *Kinds of marriage according to the occupation of the HH*

	Major	minor	Uxorilocal	Totals
A.L. (absen-	214	12	8	234
tee landlord)	91.5%	5.1%	3.4%	(23.5%)
merchant,	246	24	27	297
official-	82.8%	8.1%	9.1%	(29.8%)
artisan	123	16	16	155
	79.4%	10.3%	10.3%	(15.6%)
manual	126	21	40	187
laborer-	67.4%	11.2%	21.4%	(18.8%)
farmer	81	28	13	122
	66.4%	23.0%	10.6%	(12.3%)
totals	790	101	104	994
	79.4%	10.2%	10.4%	(100%)

$X2 = 70.57$ $X2o$ (0.5% level) $= 21.96$

The null hypothesis that difference in occupation has no relation to marriage pattern is rejected on the 0.5% level.

Table 7 compares the marriage forms found in the various occupations, to see if any form dominated in a given profession. The percentage of the major marriage form, always high in Hsinchu, declines as the classes go lower. The percentage of the minor form increases sharply amongst the 2b and 2c classes, while the percentages of uxorilocal marriages and singles is concentrated in the 2c and 3 classes. The Chi-square test against this table shows that the null hypothesis "the difference in socio-economic status has no relation to marriage form" is strongly rejected even at the 0.5% level.

The Chi-square test against Table 7 shows that the differences in occupation, indeed, revealed the greatest variation in marriage form. In the absentee landlord's case, the most dominant form was, obviously, the "standard" form. The minor form was found significant amongst the farmers, while the uxorilocal form was the highest amongst manual laborers. Between the merchant-store clerk and the artisan categories the distribution of the three kinds of marriage was quite even, showing that the average ratio of marriage forms amongst the urban residents was (i.e., a rough estimate of the ratio):

Major: minor: uxorilocal = 8: 1: 1

We are not wrong in concluding, therefore, that the occupation of the household head and therefore the socio-economic status of the family were related to the choice of marriage form.

Here, we must discuss briefly the function of the uxorilocal form of marriage, a topic neglected in the previous chapter. The status of a *chao-hsü*, or for a widow a *chao-fu*, is best defined, with great humor, in the common sense terms used by the Chinese, as a "pawned husband" or a "useless wart."[1] The purpose of obtaining an uxorilocal husband in China, according to the Chinese legal expert Shiga Shuzo, are:[2] 1) The bride's family needs a male, if there is no male offspring to a) provide a grandson, or b) support the aged and manage the family business. 2) Even if they have a male offspring, the bride's family take an uxorilocal husband for their daughter when a) their own son is useless, or b) they do not wish to see their own daughter marry out.

The situation in Taiwan was quite the same. Aneba Shohei, judge of the Taipei high court wrote:[3]

The reasons for taking a *chao-hsü* or *chao-fu* are a) to obtain working force to support the aged, b) to gain an heir (a grand- son), c) to keep as many children as possible, and d) the bride's family does not wish to see her marry out.

Both of the above law specialists, Shiga and Aneba, gave the same reason for a man to become an uxorilocal husband, that is, poverty or inability on the male's side to obtain a bride in any other form. There were, of course, exceptional cases, but the overall concept of the uxorilocal husband made it something to be avoided by the male's side. Yet if nothing worked out for the man at marriageable age, uxorilocal marriage was frequently preferred to no marriage at all.

Looking at the actual cases in the Hsinchu records, the uxorilocal marriage occurred most frequently amongst families that had no male, or had one or two boys too young to support the family. Another factor, which neither of the above law specialists stated, but the sociologist Suzuki Sei-ichiro's sharp observation noted about the uxorilocal form was that, at least in Taiwan, it was most frequently arranged for the *simpua* adopted daughters, for the above stated reasons.[4] N.b., Of the 104 cases of uxorilocal marriage in Hsinchu occurring amongst the females born between the years 1891-1920, 68 (65.4%) were of the "A" category, i.e., not related to the family.

In the cases occurring in the absentee landlord's households, only eight uxorilocal marriages were recorded over the thirty year period. Furthermore, seven of these cases were adopted males, termed here "A" category members of the absentee landlord's household. The eighth case was an absentee landlady head-of-the-house, who had just gone through a division of the household. The husband of the lady household head had died, leaving her with one offspring, a daughter.

A similar phenomenon occurs amongst the merchant and store clerk class, who marry in the uxorilocal fashion. The "O" (that is to say, consanguinal or blood-related to the family) category ratio against the "A" category here is 44.4 : 55.6 The next highest frequency of the "O" category against the "A" category occurred amongst the manual labor class, where the ratio was 37.5 : 62.5. The reason for the high frequency of the "O" ratio in the merchant class is most probably to be found in the fourth cause above, i.e. the daughter of a merchant or store clerk, being extremely skillful in managing the family business, was kept at home by the parents, who did not wish to lose her skills for the family business were she to marry out. The uxorilocal form of marriage is therefore seen to be more common for adopted rather than blood-related family members.

D. *Socio-economic status between marrying families*

In order to further understand the function of each marriage form in the city, we now turn to the next question: who marries whom? To conduct this investigation, we needed the records of a set of two families involved in one marriage. We have randomly selected 415 Northgate families in our sampling population both sides of which are traceable from 1870-1945 in the Hsinchu city registers. The distribution of the four forms of marriage in the sampling are:

Major	minor	Uxorilocal	Concubine
70.4%	14.4%	6.3%	8.9%

Regarding the concubine form of marriage, which was not included in the earlier examination, the distribution of the four forms of marriage, even with the statistics for concubines included, was more or less constant over the period studied, i.e., people born from 1891 to 1945. Based on the classification of five economic statuses, a test was done in order to determine which class married with which class, and what form was more likely to occur in each class.

Table 8 shows that the standard form (Major) had the highest percentage in marriages between families of the same socio-economic class. Minor and uxorilocal forms had concentrated rates in the category of brides marrying with lower status grooms, while the contrary was observed in the concubine form. I.e., concubine marriages almost always occurred between a male of higher socio-economic status and a women of lesser economic means. Only two of the concubine marriages studied were with men of lower status than the woman.

Table 8. *Comparison of statuses of two families involved in each form of marriage* (wife marrying status:)

	same	down	up	total
Major	139	95	58	292
	47.6%	32.5%	19.9%	(70.4%)
minor	21	31	8	60
	35%	51.5%	13.3%	(14.4%)
Uxorilocal	7	16	3	26
	26.9%	61.5%	11.5%	(6.3%)
Concubine	13	2	22	37
	35.1%	5.4%	59.5%	(8.9%)
Totals	180	144	91	415
	43.4%	34.7%	21.9%	(100%)

$X2 = 52.5$ $X2o$ (0.5% level) = 18.55

The null hypothesis that the socio-economic status difference between the two families had no relationship to marriage pattern is rejected on the 0.5% level by the Chi-square test.

Table 9.1. *Comparison of girl's status in the previous household (before marriage) according to four types of marriage.*

	"O" category	"A" category	Totals
Major	188	104	292
	64.4%	35.6%	(70.2%)
minor	44	16	60
	73.3%	26.7%	(14.4%)
Uxorilocal	8	18	26
	30.8%	69.2%	(6.3%)
Concubine	8	29	37
	21.6%	78.4%	(8.9%)
Totals	248	167	415
	59.8%	40.2%	(100%)

$X2 = 31.04$ $X2o$ (0.05% level) = 12.84

The null hypothesis that the difference in the girl's status has no relation to marriage pattern is rejected at 0.5% level.

Tables 9.1 tests if there was any correlation between the woman's position within the family and the form of marriage, i.e., between the "O" category and the "A" category (i.e., blood related or non-related family member). In principle, we believe that the minor form should not have had such a high level (26.7%) in the "A" category. The reason for this has to be carefully examined later, but our tentative interpretation is that there were quite a few "adopted" daughters whom the foster parents had no plan to marry to one of their sons, but had to do so simply because an unexpected union of the two had occurred. Before pursuing the question further, Table 9.2 must be studied.

Table 9.2. *Male status in major and minor forms of marriage.*

	"O" category	"A" category	Totals
Major	187	105	292
	64.0%	36.0%	(83.0%)
minor	29	31	60
	48.3%	51.7%	(17.0%)
Totals	216	136	352
	61.4%	38.6%	(100%)

X2 = 7.6   Xo (1% level) = 6.63

The null hypothesis that difference in boy's status has no relation to marriage patterns is rejected on the 1% level.

Another possible reason for the high number of minor marriages in the "A" category can be seen in Table 9.2. The parents did not mind marrying their twice "adopted" daughter with their "adopted" son. Thus, of the males who married in the minor form, more than 50% of them belonged to the "A" category. Some extreme cases show that the only reason for the foster parents to "adopt" a son was to marry him with their already "adopted" daughter. In such cases, the groom-to-be was "adopted" in at marriageable age, while the *t'ung-yang-hsi* (*simpua*) or the *yang-nü* turned *t'ung-yang-hsi* had been raised since young. This is of course closer to the uxorilocal form of marriage than to the minor, yet the groom-to-be's family or the groom-to-be himself saved the family's face, having avoided the stigma of being classified a "pawned" or useless uxorilocal husband.

103

In the next table, the difference in the degrees of social gaps between the two families are tested, according to the form of marriage. Marriages of two partners within the same socio-economic class, or separated either upward or downward by one class are listed under category #1. Marriages between families separated by two steps or more are classified as category #2.

Table10.1. *Degrees of status gap according to four types of marriage.*

	same or 1 step	2 steps or more	totals
Major	225	67	292
	77.1%	22.9%	(70.4%)
minor	36	24	60
	60.0%	40.0%	(14.4%)
Uxorilocal	15	11	26
	57.7%	42.3%	(6.3%)
Concubine	18	19	37
	48.6%	51.4%	(8.9%)
Totals	294	121	415
	70.8%	29.2%	(100%)

$X2 = 19.31$ $\qquad$ $X2o$ (0.5% level) = 12.84

The null hypothesis that the degrees of status gap between the two families has no relation to marriage form is rejected on the 0.5% level.

Thus the standard form of marriage occurred mainly between two families of the same or close social status. In other words, it was very common for an absentee landlord family to take a bride from another absentee landlord, while the coolie family was more likely to take a bride from a rickshaw dealer. There were, however, many exceptions to the rule, since the city had so many more possibilities and social positions than did the farming-rural community.

The minor marriage, on the other hand, had a different class breakdown, as can be seen in the following Table 10.2. The social gap between the bride marrying in the minor fashion and her husband's family increased significantly according to the lower social status of the family contracting a minor marriage. I.e., *simpua* girls who married a boy from a high class family were usually of a higher social status, while

104

girls from a lower economic group had a 60% chance, when marrying in the minor fashion, of entering a higher financial status.:

Table 10.2. *Minor marriage according to socio-economic status.*

socio-economic status	same or one step	two or more steps
1	100%	0
2a	88.8%	11.2%
2b	62.5%	37.5%
2c	53.3%	46.7%
3	40%	60%

In the case of the Grade 1 family, there were only five minor marriages observed. Of the five, four took a *simpua* or "minibride" from another Grade 1 family, while the one family who were Hakka took a mini-bride from a Grade 2a family. Focusing on the standard form of marriage, we then measured the status gap in all marriages.

Table 11. *Comparison of degrees of status gap, according to socio-economic station, in major marriage*

Class	same or 1 step	2 steps or more	totals
1	67	7	74
	90.5%	9.5%	(25.3%)
2a	68	12	80
	85.0%	15.0%	27.4%
2b	35	15	50
	70.0%	30.0%	17.1%
2c	34	14	48
	70.8%	29.2%	16.4%
3	21	19	40
	52.5%	47.5%	13.7%
totals	225	67	292
	77.1%	22.9%	(100%)

$X2 = 27.47$ $X2o$ (0.5% level) = 14.86

The null hypothesis that the difference in degrees of status gap has no relation to socio-economic status is rejected on the 0.5% level.

Table 11 shows that an overwhelming 90.5% of Grade 1 families took a bride from the same or the next closest status (2a), while as the socio-economic status went lower, the gap between the two categories (same or 1 step, and 2 or more steps) came closer. Lower status families managed to obtain a bride in the standard form from a higher status family rather easily in the city, since there were plentiful girls in the urban setting. (N.b., Hsinchu city and county had a higher ratio of females to males than other parts of Taiwan. The 1930 census shows females 100 : males 105.6 for all Taiwan, while Hsinchu city was the reverse: females 100 : males 96). or the families of 2c or 3 social status the best way to obtain a higher status bride was to take her as a *simpua*, or marry out a son as an uxorilocal husband.

But plentiful girls in this case means mainly the "A" category girls of a high status family. When marriage occurred between two extremely different statuses, there seem to have been a number of other reasons besides the ones discussed above. By re-examining the records in each case, our study of the household registers shows that marriages tended to occur between disparate statuses when:

Case type1. The address of the two families is either very close or exactly the same, including those places where groom-to-be or bride-to-be resided in the household of the parents-to-be as an employee or a lodger before marriage.

Case type 2. A bride-to-be was pregnant before the wedding.

Case type 3. There was some sort of affiliation between the two families, either through marriage of an older member or through business relationships.

Summary

As the tables indicated clearly, the dominant form of marriage in Hsinchu city was the "standard" (Major) form. It was not that the city had fewer *t'ung-yang-hsi* (*simpua*) or *yang-nü*, but rather that fewer boys of the city families actually married with the *t'ung-yang* girl in the minor fashion. The promise of marriage exchanged between two sets of parents was more likely to be carried to completion in a rural rather than in a more impersonal urban setting.

Also well known is the fact that there were two kinds of *t'ung-yang-hsi* or *yang-nü*, definitely distinguished in the people's minds. One kind was "bought" and the other was "given."[5] Our Chinese associates of Hsinchu, who were immensely helpful throughout the study, all agree to the point that there were more "bought" girls in the urban setting than in the rural area.[6] If a girl was "bought," her relationship with her natal family was severed. If a girl was "given," the relationship grew between the two families to that of *ch'in-ch'i* affinal association -- the same sort of relationship engendered by the standard form of marriage.

The uxorilocal form of marriage was chosen for the male in the city setting under various circumstances. Yet as Table 5 indicated, the males in the lower class households had the highest percentage of this less prestigious form of marriage. Also obvious was the uxorilocal male's lower social status (*shen-fen*) in the framework of the family. Unlike the minor form, it was often a brother, nephew, cousin of the household head, or even a single household head himself who married in the uxorilocal form. This seems to indicate that those who had lost their father at an earlier stage of their life, had more probability of becoming an uxorilocal husband, than those who had a family to look after their marital interests.

There are many more interesting details that can be discussed from the above sets of statistics. The categories used to test the data reflect the complexity of the Chinese family structure, especially when the data are presented for process analysis. To make the best use of our data, so rich in information, an approach is indeed needed that adjusts to the many forms of marriage patterns, whose basic purpose is to establish the very center of social and cultural life, the Chinese family. The openness of Chinese social custom to adaptation and change, according to the exigencies the particular situation, is indeed the key to understanding the complexities of marriage in the frontier life of Taiwan, as well as in the labor-intensive industrialization of modern times. With the arrival of economic affluence, the minor and to a lesser degree uxorilocal marriage forms have died out. We can only admire the openness of a family system that can survive all challenges to its centrality, whether frontier, capitalist, or socialist in origin.

Notes

1. See Niida, Noboru, *Shina Mibun Hoshi (The Laws of Social Status in China)*, Tokyo: Toyo Bunka, 1942, p. 732. The uxorilocal husband did not have the right of inheritance or of authority over his own children unless they bore his family name, as confirmed by Aneba Shohei, *Tokushu Horitsu ni Tsuite (The Special Customary Laws of China)*, Taipei: 1934, pp. 631 and 622, lines 6-8.

2. Shiga, Shuzo, *Chugoku Kazoku Ho no Genri (The Origins of Chinese Family Law)*, Tokyo: Sobunsha, 1976, p. 731.

3. Aneba, P. 621. lines 6-8.

4. Suzuki, Sei-ichiro, *Kan, Kon, So, Sai, to Nenju Gyogi (Rites of Passage and Annual Festivals)*, Taipei: 1934, p. 140, line 8.

5. Aneba, p. 636. "Though the Chinese in Taiwan make a clear distinction between the bought and given *simpua*, the (Japanese) government does not recognize it legally."

6. Chinese informants questioned in Beijing, Hopei, Nanjing, Ch'eng-tu, and Shanghai report seeing *t'ung-yang-hsi* in wealthy households up to the Socialist period.

7. RETHINKING CHINESE FAMILY STRUCTURE
(Charts by Susan Moriyama)

An analysis of the Chinese family through its marriage forms, provided by Nariko Akimoto in chapter 6, yields important statistical evidence to show the wide variety of means available to establish the family, the basic and essential unit of Chinese society. Eighty-four percent of the urban families of Hsinchu city chose the traditional form of marriage to establish the family in Hsinchu city. The choice of the minor bride (child adopted to be a future bride) stood at 11% and uxorilocal husbands at 5% throughout the first 76 years (1870-1946) of our study, and dwindled to a negligible percent in the last 24 years, as seen in the 1970-1976 registers supplied by Marta Levitt.

Furthermore, each of the families studied, other circumstances not preventing, went from the nuclear, through the extended, to the grand family form over the 100 year period. In other words, the ideal Chinese family, i.e., three generations (grandparents, parents, and children) under a single roof, or behind a single household entrance, was realized by the majority of the families who lived in the urban setting of Hsinchu.

The fact that the ideal and the real Chinese family coincided in this frontier township, noted for its conservative ways, was true for the majority of families interviewed in chapters 2-5 of our study, from various provinces throughout China. Why it was the rule must extend beyond purely economic and material causes (i.e., the wealth and the space required to build the grand family). It is in our judgment a true cultural constant, presupposed at the structural or subconscious level of Chinese family life, that parents, children, and grandparents in a single household represent an economically and socially practical way to conduct family life in the Chinese living environment. Such a conclusion becomes more obvious as one resides for longer periods of time within the Chinese city, as participants in household and public festival, rituals of life's passages, and the daily needs of running a merchant, artist, or worker's household.

The majority of the households in the central part of the city, represented by the Northgate and Westgate family registers, live behind a storefront or family business. Shop fronts in the old Chinese city were in fact entrances to households in our registers. Both the household head and his wife, their relatives (sometimes listed as "lodgers") and older children worked in the family business located at the street level. Grandparents watched over the grandchildren in the courtyards and back rooms of the family residence. A second, third, and sometimes fourth floor above the street level housed the extended and grand family members. Thus the physical and economic needs of the household business actually promoted the need for building the extended and grand family systems.

City households that extended beyond the marketing center of the city, and did not have shops at street level, i.e., were true residences of the merchants, landlords, and wealthier town members, were also constructed with the functional purpose in mind of building the grand family. Unlike the sprawling farming communities of the suburbs, which added a new room or *fang* each time a son was married, the city houses could only build upward as the family grew in size. The second and third floors of the city dwellings were built out over the sidewalks, providing shade from the summer heat, and protection from winter rains to passerby, as well as extra rooms for the expanding family. Businesses prospered in direct proportion to the size of the family. All of life, social, economic, religious, and material, depended upon the realization of the family ideal.

The following charts re-examine the statistical tables of chapter 6 as bar graphs, to show how families were formed, from the colonial period into modernity. Major marriage was preferred for city dwellers, while minor and uxorilocal marriages occurred, for the most part, between couples who moved into the city from outside, or were not directly related by blood to the household in which the marriage occurred. We see that a little less than half of the uxorilocal marriages happened between *simpua* girls adopted into the family, and a *ming-ling-tzu* boy adopted from outside the clan. From these facts we conclude that major marriage was the predominant social ritual for establishing the family. Minor and uxorilocal marriages were for those members who could not otherwise be provided for. In the case of modern china, family remains central to social and cultural life.

By analyzing the statistics of chapter 5 as graphic bar charts, we see clearly the process of change towards the "traditional" form of major marriage, and away from the minor and uxorilocal forms. As Hsinchu moved towards economic modernization, *simpua* adoption decreased dramatically with the coming of the new market economy.

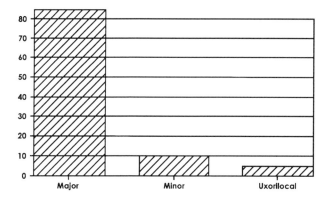

Chart 1. The percentage of marriages occurring in Hsinchu city, 1910-1946.

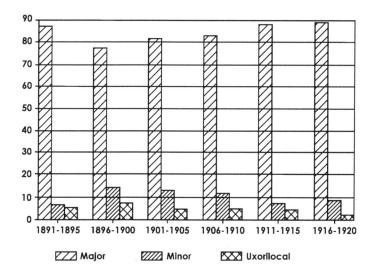

Chart 2. The proportion of Major to minor and uxorilocal marriage, 1911-1946.

Next, we must ask 1) whether or not the increase in population, both by birth and by movement into the city affected marriage patterns, and 2) whether or not minor and uxorilocal marriages are a factor of social and economic status.

In the following charts we see that 1) the kind of marriage is definitely a function of socio-economic status, and 2) birth in the clan or family vs. movement into the city or family are also determining factors in the kind of marriage chosen to form a family.

By comparing the household head's occupation with the city tax records, chapter 3 defined five kinds of socio-economic status. These are: 1) absentee landlords, and other elite gentry families; 2a) wealthy entrepreneurs; 2b) middle class merchants, shop owners; 2c) clerical staff, farmers, artisans; and 3) coolies, hard labor. Chart 3 displays the percentage of major, minor, and uxorilocal marriages occurring in each of the five socio-economic categories between 1911 and 1946. Minor marriages are highest in the farming and labor class, while uxorilocal marriages are frequent amongst the labor-coolie class.

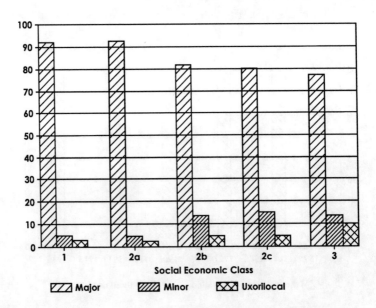

Chart 3. Kinds of marriage entered into according to the socio-economic status of the family head, 1911-1946.

Chart 3 brings us to a clearer understanding of the role wealth and status have in deciding the kind of marriage chosen to form a nuclear family. By far the greater number of minor marriages (i.e., of the family head to a *simpua* girl acquired at a tender age to eventually marry a son of the family) occur in middle class merchants, farmers, and laborer households.

An even clearer distinction is seen in the case of the uxorilocal marriage. The husbands chosen in the majority of cases are from the lowest coolie working class. In all five socio-economic categories, the major form of marriage is the dominant form in city life. But if the minor and uxorilocal forms are chosen, the economic factor seems to be crucial in deciding the kind of husband or bride chosen.

Chart 4 examines the kind of marriage chosen according to the occupation of the household head. In it we see even more clearly that the uxorilocal form of marriage is highest for manual laborers, while the minor marriage is highest for farmers.

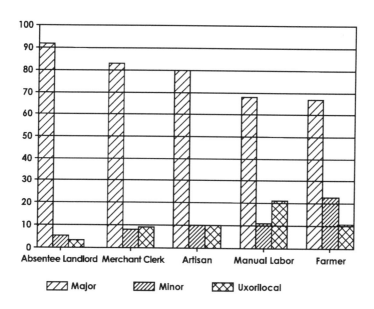

Chart 4. Marriages of the landlord class compared to 2c merchants, clerks, farmers, and Grade 3 laborers.

113

A far smaller number of *simpua* girls are actually married in the minor fashion, than those "adopted" as future brides. Of those who do marry into the family, 12 - 17% are seen to be pregnant before the marriage is registered, which suggests that the number of minor marriages may have been less for the city statistics, had an unforeseen liaison not occurred.

We noted earlier that minor and uxorilocal marriages are more frequently arranged for adopted members of the household, or relatives who have moved in from the countryside as lodgers, even though related consanguinally to a family member (the "A" category of chapter 3).

Using computer graphics, we isolated all major, minor, and uxorilocal marriages occurring between 1911 and 1946, according to males who were born in ("O" category), adopted or moved into a Hsinchu household (the "A" category). Chart 5 shows the results of the inquiry:

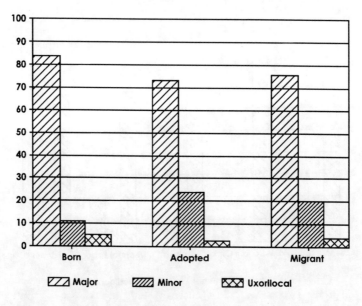

Chart 5. Kinds of marriage according to household status: born ("O"), or adopted/moved in ("A"), 1911-1946.

Chart 5 shows conclusively that minor marriages occurred most frequently for adopted and temporary lodgers in the urban household. That is, the less prestigious form of marriage to a *simpua* girl adopted at a tender age occurred either to non-members of the household (a *ming-ling-tzu* adopted son not related to the family) or to a distant relative who was listed as a "lodger" in the city dwelling, for whom the cost of a wedding was not subsumed by his (or her) own family. The uxorilocal form of marriage, on the other hand, was slightly higher for the temporary lodger who was a distant relative of the household.

The charts show that the major form of marriage was the predominant form for all new families established within the city. The less prestigious minor and uxorilocal forms were more liable to occur for household members of lower family status.

A further analysis, based on the number of concubine marriages that occurred after major marriage, yields further insight into the form of marriage and socio-economic status. We turn again to the graphic chart to ask, first, how many major marriages were later followed by a concubine relationship (i.e., record of paternity occurrences to other than a first wife), and then measure the social gap between bride and groom for the four kinds of marriage. That is, we shall first ask how many concubine marriages occurred between 1911 and 1946. We shall then measure the socio-economic gap, if any, between the households forming a marriage alliance.

Concubine marriage, it must be noted, lessens the percentage of major marriages recorded in chart 1. This is because concubine marriage occurred, for the most part, in households which had first contracted a major marriage, and were affluent enough to afford a later concubine relationship. The concubine marriage as a distinct classification did not, however, significantly change the percentage of minor or uxorilocal marriages.

The reason for choosing minor marriages compared to the uxorilocal and concubine forms, can be understood from the status gap between minor brides and their husbands. A full 60% of the minor marriages entered on in Hsinchu city occurred in families where the *simpua* bride was two economic steps below the family she entered into, thus assuring a step upward in economic status for the bride.

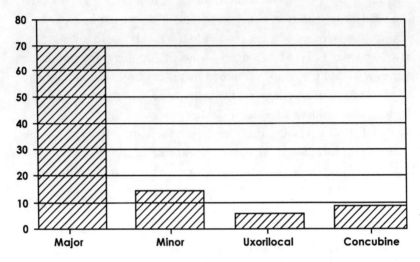

Chart 6. Comparison of marriages in Hsinchu, 1911-1946.

Concubine marriages occurred in 9% of the household registers of Hsinchu city, a phenomenon noted by the Chinese character *chieh* in the city records. A concubine's child is by the law of social status (*shen-fen*) entitled to a share in the family estate, upon the death of the male listed in the registers as parent. An illegitimate child on the other hand (*szu-Sheng-tzu* in the household register) is by legal definition registered without a male parent's name. The illegitimate child is entitled to a share of the household estate if the mother is listed as a household head.

These legal distinctions are of great importance in deciding court cases, and thus are carefully recorded in the household registers. As noted in chapter two, the concubine marriage created special problems for the Japanese courts during the colonial period (1895-1945). The problem was solved by recording all births that might otherwise have been illegitimate as a concubine (*chieh*) marriage in the household registers, based on the recognition of paternity at the time of entry in the records. The dissolution of a concubine relationship, allowing the

116

woman to marry in the major fashion, was not called a divorce (li-*hun*) but rather the dissolution of a legal contract (li-*yüan*).

The inclusion of concubine marriages in our statistics adds a new dimension to the study of the Chinese family system. Concubine marriages are not limited to, but tend to occur most frequently in the higher economic brackets. The reasons for maintaining the concubine relationship include the following: 1) the first wife is barren, or only produces female offspring, prompting the household head to seek a second or third liaison in order to have more offspring. 2) The city's business associations, i.e., the merchant and landlord classes, frequent the courtesan houses and bars, and either sponsor or have an affair with a courtesan. 3) The laws of the southeast Asian nations in which overseas Chinese reside only allow native citizens to own land. The first and second reasons for taking a concubine are dominant in the Hsinchu household registers.

In the following charts, we examine the social gap between bride and groom, in marriages occurring between 1911 and 1946.

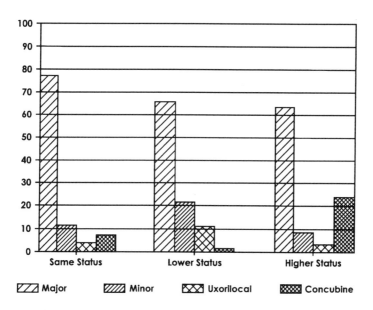

Chart 7. Marriage patterns of grooms, by social status.

Chart 7 shows that the proportion of males who married in the minor and uxorilocal fashion to brides of lower status was high, while males who married a concubine were usually from a higher social status than the second wife. We notice again that in all cases, the number of city males marrying in the major fashion was higher than all other forms of marriage. It is also evident that a slightly higher percentage of males married women of higher status, a statistic that will be tested in the following set of charts.

In chart 8 we examine the percentage of women marrying men of the same, lower, and higher status. Here it is obvious that women who married in the uxorilocal fashion took males of a lower socio-economic status, while concubines for the most part were of a lower status than their lovers-husbands. Since minor marriages are not analyzed by economic, "A" or "O" status, the percentage of minor brides for men of lower status seems higher than in fact it is, for which compare chart 9.

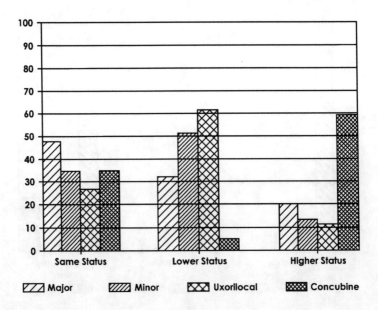

Chart 8. Marriage & social status for women, 1911-1946.

Whereas the percentage of women marrying men of lower status is noticeably higher in the minor and uxorilocal form, an overwhelming number of the concubine marriages are seen to be with men of the higher socio-economic brackets. That these figures are predictable and self-fulfilling, if considered in the light of the traditional Chinese value system that places the creation of a nuclear family the most important duty incumbent on the young couple, and marriage in any form allowable in order that the nuclear family be generated, is in fact a premature conclusion. Far more social and cultural forces are at work than indicated by the statistics found in the registers.

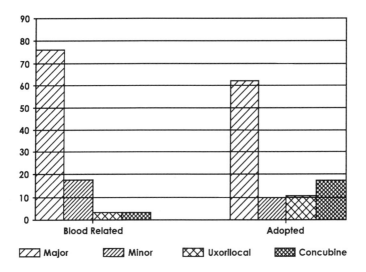

Chart 9. Female marriages according to family origin.

Chart 9 re-examines the status of the females who marry in the city, according to the "O" and "A" categories defined in chapter 3. That is, Major, minor, uxorilocal, and concubine marriages are sorted for all females in the Hsinchu household registers who marry between 1911 and 1946. The chart gives even more striking evidence the lower status marriages arranged for girls as well as boys not related by blood to the household head. We again affirm that a higher proportion of adopted girls are married in the uxorilocal and concubine fashion, than girls who are related consanguinally to the household head.

We also note, surprisingly, that 10.5% of the minor marriages are arranged for girls who are first adopted into one family, then adopted out again to another family as a minor bride. Some minor marriages are arranged for girls who are twice adopted, i.e., sold as *simpua* brides to a third family after being adopted in from a farming family outside the city precincts. We further note that a higher percentage of concubine marriages are entered into by girls adopted into the city, who subsequently work in the city bars or courtesan "night-life" trade.

The statistics shown in Chart 9 are even more dramatically displayed when we create a bar graph showing the percentage of all marriages individually, (i.e., within each category), according to blood relationship or adoption with the household head. Chart 10 shows that the uxorilocal and concubine forms of marriage were most frequently arranged for girls adopted in to the city family from unrelated families. A much higher percentage of blood related girls are adopted out as *simpua* child brides-to-be than are equivalent marriages arranged for boys.

The bar graph generated in Chart 10 gives dramatic evidence of the preferences of the city families for marriages that conform to

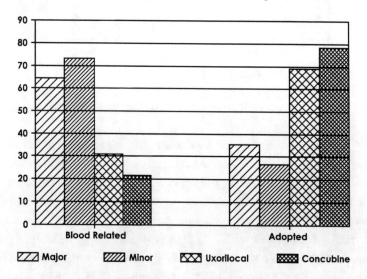

Chart 10. Overall percentage of female marriages
by relationship to the household head.

traditionally accepted socio-economic status. The majority of the major marriages that occurred in the city registers were for girls consanguinally related to the household head, whereas 78% of the concubine marriages were entered upon by women who were not related, i.e., were lodgers or unrelated by blood to the household in which they lived.

Only 72% of the *simpua* who actually married in the minor fashion were married to a son of the family after a first adoption. 28% of the minor marriages occurred after a second adoption, that is, the *simpua* girl was sold again to establish ties within the city network of merchants. Other *simpua* were found to be pregnant before marriage, and sent away from their first adopting family to be married in another.

If we compare the figures found in Chart 10 with the percentage of males married in the major and minor fashion, the contrast between male and female status within the family is more than evident. 88% of grooms related to the household head were married in the major fashion, while only 12% were married to *simpua* brides. 78% of the non-related grooms were married in the Major fashion, while 22% were provided with minor marriages. The relationship to the household head was a determining factor in deciding the kind of marriage.

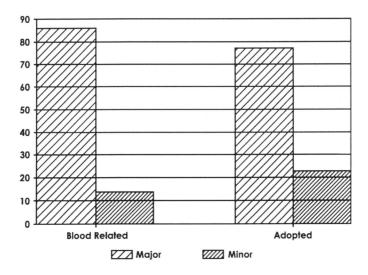

Chart 11. Male marriages, by relationship to the HH.

121

Conclusion of the Statistical Section

Studying the kinds of marriage available in the Chinese system to form the nuclear family, as found in the Hsinchu household registers gives convincing evidence of the preference for traditional values, i.e., the major marriage, for both related and non-related inhabitants of the city household. When minor and uxorilocal marriages as well as concubine relationships were invoked to create the nuclear family, these less prestigious forms of marriage tended to occur more frequently among the non-related or non-city members of the Chinese family.

The detailed analysis of the urban Chinese family and its structure, which did not change significantly from the late nineteenth century Ch'ing period to the modern industrial twentieth century, was possible because of the vivid description given us by the Household registers. The Hsinchu statistics seem to typify the Chinese ideal, analogous to the studies of Okuda, Suzuki, Niida Noboru, Sophie Sa, and other studies of mainland, southeast and north China communities.

A final conclusion to be drawn from our charts, is to affirm that the more affluent the Chinese family became, that is, as it approached the modern industrial present, the more conservative did marriage form become. By the 1970's when our study began, there were almost no minor marriages, and very few uxorilocal alliances recorded in the modern city household registers.

The modern Chinese family continues to be the very center of Chinese socio-economic life, providing the basis for cultural as well as economic survival. The fact that another 11-12% of the registers recorded single, female household heads who adopted children to create a family, demonstrate that without relatives or familial relationships of some sort, life in the Chinese community is difficult if not impossible.

8. CONCLUSION:
FAMILY VALUES IN MODERN CHINA

To what extent the values of traditional family life have survived into the present is a moot point. One of the first problems presented to our study was how to evaluate the modern family objectively, so that scholars as well as ordinary readers would find our data and conclusions useful for understanding something about the new China. If one relies solely on the Household Registers, a very cut-and-dry, albeit infinitely detailed picture is clearly given of a single city in SE China. If, on the other hand, the evidence hinges solely on the very human and feeling-filled anecdotes of chapters 2-4, the extent to which the data presented is valid cannot extend further than the individual family that told its own tale.

My choice of methodology for testing the significance of the values and ideas expressed by the modern Chinese families interviewed, was an adapted form of the Thematic Apperceptive Test (TAT), which was developed and utilized over a two year period by a variety of American and Filipino(a) scholars at the Ateneo de Manila between 1961-62. The test was designed by Dr. Frank Lynch, S.J., Ph.D., Anthropology, Dr. Emy Paschasio, Ph.D. linguistics, John McCarron, S.J., Ph.D. Linguistics, Jaime Bulatao, S.J., Ph.D. Psychology, and Mary Racelis, Ph.D. Sociology.

In this test (updated in 1998), five pictures were shown to a total of 300 American students and 300 Filipino students. The pictures were: 1) a family, consisting of mother, father, and child; 2) a Caucasian couple dancing; 3) men and women around a table listening to a woman give a report; 4) a room with young men and women studying or reading books; 5) western style food on a table. Each person taking the test was asked to write a brief story about what was happening in the picture. I was directed, as a research assistant to the team of scholars, to count the number of words most frequently recurring in the stories. The results of the test were published in the Ateneo de Manila Annuarium in 1962, and other journals.

I began using this test during our initial family study from 1972-1974 in Taiwan. I used it again at the University of Hawaii, from

1974 through 1986, a period of twelve years, during which time approximately 100 persons a semester, or 200 students per academic year, responded with brief stories concerning the five pictures. The pictures themselves were re-drawn by artists in the Audio-visual department of the University of Hawai'i, making a standardized set of images shown to 2,400 students over the twelve year period.

The ethnic or cultural composition of the students tested at the University of Hawai'i was very wide. Chinese informants included students from mainland China, Singapore, Hongkong, Taiwan, and Americans of Chinese ancestry. Japanese from Japan and Americans of Japanese ancestry, Koreans, Filipino(a), Vietnamese, Hawai'ian, Tongan, Samoan, Native American, Caucasian and Afro-American students, also chose to write TAT stories as part of their out-of-class volunteer assignments. The statistics of the test were made public each semester, and used by the students to write their own assessments of our findings. Since there is no "majority" ethnic group in Hawai'i, it was possible to get a very extensive picture of how young men and women in their late teens and early twenties responded to the TAT pictures.

Not all social scientists consider the results of TAT data to be conclusive. Whatever problems are associated with the TAT aside, the results of the University of Hawai'i survey were most useful in giving some insight into the differences, if nothing else, between the Chinese students and other cultural responses to the pictures.

The most commonly recurring words (over 60% response per story), by place of origin, were as follows:

1) *Chinese students*, born in China or overseas:

family: children must respect their parents, look after them when they get old.

date: the young couple are engaged, about to be married.

meeting: to earn money in business is the highest goal.

class: study hard; to be a financial success in business is, important.

food: desire to eat good Chinese food.

2) *Japanese students*, born in Japan, 60% and above response:

family: students away from home studying miss their family.

date: I may have an affair with a westerner, but will marry a Japanese.

124

meeting: after graduation, one must get a job in a good company in Japan.

class: high school students studying to pass the college entrance exams.

food: desire to eat good Japanese food, preference for Sushi.

The majority of Asian students, Chinese, Japanese, Korean, and Filipino(a) gave overwhelmingly positive responses to family values, mentioning family in all five pictures.

3) *Mainland American students*, ethnicity non specific.

family: mixed response. "Drop the child and see if it bounces."
"throw the child in a swimming pool and see if it swims," "I wanted to get away from home during college," "I'm working, don't ask folks for money;" "toothpaste advertisement."

date: Boy and girl on a date. He hopes she's willing to make love after the dance.

meeting: Women are assuming management roles in business.

class: If a student studies hard, he or she will get an "A."

food: We must watch what we eat, not put on weight, stay healthy.

Though the American responses seemed at first flippant, later class discussion showed that "humor" rather than true objective feelings were expressed in the students' TAT stories.

The Ateneo de Manila study published in 1962 listed the number of value words repeated most frequently in the TAT responses. Using this model, we found the following most frequently occurring phrases/themes in the TAT stories:

a) *Chinese students*: (most frequently occurring words in responses to pictures 1 thru 5, in order of occurrence):
1) earn money in business; 2) success through *Guanxi* relationships; 3) obligation to family and friends; 4) *shenfen*, social status brings power and influence; 5) enjoy good food.

b) *Japanese students:* 1) *kimochi* feelings towards the picture; 2) *omoiyari*, sensitivity to feelings; 3) *amae, amaete iru*, desire for self-indulgence, satisfy desires; 4) college education means a higher salary; 5) enjoy good food.

c) *Filipino students:* 1) *sa awa ng dios,* by God's will, or by society's approval; 2) *pakikisama,* sensitivity to others feelings; 3) *sa utang na loob,* sense of obligation for favors or gifts received; 4) *hiya,* sense of shame or obligation to perform well for family's face and social status; 5) desire for good food.

d) *American born students*: 1) hard work brings success; 2) social acceptance by peer group; 3) upward mobility through earned wealth; 4) humor (seen in the responses to the five TAT pictures); 5) concern for health maintenance by good diet.

It was not so much the statistical results derived from a word count of the responses, as the dialogue and written essays generated after the results were published, which produced a much deeper understanding amongst the students of their varied cultural dissimilarities. Chinese students were very explicit about explaining the meaning of *hsiao (xiao)* parent-child relationships in stories, and subsequent explanatory essays, even though the word *xiao* did not occur that frequently in the TAT stories. Japanese students, on the other hand, stated a clear preference for a Japanese style marriage and family, in response to the picture of dating.

Perhaps most interesting of all was the response of the mainland educated American students, who, knowing that their stories would be analyzed in class, did their best to be humorous in their responses, winning obvious acclaim and some sense of recognition before their peer group.

The test was of immense value as a heuristic device to make a multi-ethnic group of students much more interested in dissecting, analyzing, and explaining their differences, and understanding each other during and outside of class discussions.

The main use of the test, for the purpose of my family study, however, lay not in the answers given by the students, but in the lengthy written responses of parents, senior citizens, and other adults who saw the results of the study brought home by their children, and discussed with them their own version of cultural values and roots. I soon found parents attending my lectures on Chinese cultural values, festivals, and family studies, and deciding on their own to write out and give to me their reactions to my findings. The TAT responses, when explained to an audience of mature, professional adults, generated page-after-page of feedback from people who took the project far more seriously than

126

the students. I shall recap one such response here, which is representative in a very moving way, of how Chinese view foreigners' attempts to live in their family-and-friend-oriented environment on a daily basis.

The event I have chosen to relate occurred in 1962, after the first year of the TAT study and analysis at the Ateneo de Manila. Its beginnings, however, extend two years back in time to the winter of 1959-61, when I spent every Thursday and Saturday diving off the shores of Lingayen Gulf, the island of Luzon, in the Philippines, with a close Chinese friend and classmate, who was himself a rigorous scientist. I shall call him Andy, for the purpose of the narrative.

Together we collected 512 species of tropical sea shells, and 125 specimens of coral for the Observatory collection on Mt. Mirador, Baguio city, in the mountains of north Luzon.

Andy was from a small village in Hepei (Hebei) province, north China. He was sent abroad to study in 1949, just before liberation by the Eighth Route Army in north China. He had not heard from his family for more than ten years. Then in late 1959 letters started to come again, asking for food after the disastrous Great Leap Forward in 1958.

During the many days spent diving along the reefs off Bauang and San Fernando, La Union district, Andy talked frequently of his childhood, his parents, and especially of the relationship between him, and his siblings with his mother. "A Chinese mother is not allowed to hug her older sons, or show open affection such as you do in the west," he told me. "I always loved it when I had the flu, or felt ill, because then my mother would press her cheek against mine, to see if I had a fever. It was as if her warmth made me better."

Typhoons that blew across the Pacific, carrying life-bearing rain to the rice paddy of south China, were especially violent from May through October in Baguio. One night in late October, when winds were blustering violently against our study window, a small brown bird with a bright blue moon-shaped crescent on its chest was blown flat against the pane. Andy reached carefully out the window, deftly caught the bird, and kept it in his room that night until it could be safely released the next morning to continue its journey southward.

127

It was a migratory bird found only in Hepei Province, he told me, from his home in Xianxian county, on the Shandong border with Hepei. His classmates from north China all came to his room to see the bird. They were deeply moved, some even crying to recognize something from home.

Soon after that incident, in December of 1960, I did something, I am not sure what, to offend Andy. For two years we continued to do research and collect shells together, but from that time on he never spoke to me or related any more details of his home life in Hepei province.

Then in the spring of 1962 I was asked to address the student body of our college on the TAT study of Ateneo de Manila, and its usefulness in understanding Chinese culture. I spoke of family values, friendship, loyalty, and other phrases that occurred frequently in stories as the Chinese participants in the TAT responded. How easy it was for foreigners such as myself to give offense in Asia, without knowing the reason why, I stated. Perhaps a careful study of the TAT stories could help foreigners understand about China, and Chinese understand the complexity and enigma of foreigners who come to China.

After my talk another classmate came to my room, a mathematician from Shanghai, who was friends with both Andy and myself. I shall call him Frank for the purpose of the story. Frank told me that I had, indeed, deeply offended Andy. It was due to a variety of causes that an offense, once given in China, could never be forgiven.

I felt despondent, but Frank then assured me that there was in fact a way to lessen the seriousness of the offense. I was elated to be instructed further. After much discussion, we made the following plan.

Frank, who was higher in status than either of us socially, i.e., in *shen-fen* or social rank (he said), would announce to all our Chinese classmates, Shanghai and northerners, that I, Lao Su (Michael Saso) was going to give a banquet in honor of Andy, to thank him for all the years of close cooperation. "Be sure and have boiled *chiao-tzu* (*jiaozi*, hand-wrapped Chinese style ravioli), because northerners like this dish better than anything, whereas Shanghai and other southerners preferred the more subtle and refined flavors of wonton soup," he instructed me. I decided to provide both chiao-tzu and wonton, for Frank.

128

I prepared a huge picnic lunch, catering some of the dishes, and asking the other northerners from Hepei province to come and help me make chiao-tzu. Promptly at noon we served a huge Chinese banquet on the slopes of Mt. Mirador, looking out over the vast expanse of the Pacific, knowing that China lay just over the horizon beyond the distant view of Lingayen gulf. There was plenty of wine and merriment at the banquet. Everyone volunteered to sing a song of some sort or other. They all seemed to know that this was my way of apologizing to, as well as thanking Andy.

After finishing lunch and cleaning up the hillside, I returned to my room to take a siesta. There was a quiet knock at my door. I opened it, to find Andy waiting there to see me. He had prepared three pages of notes, all written in Chinese, to explain the many ways in which I had given offense by my insensitive, foreign behavior. He was quite serious.

I was, to say the least, delighted beyond measure, and invited Andy to go over the list with a magnifying glass, and translate it immediately into English. The results of that translation, some three pages in close typed English, were later boiled down to the brief summary that appears here below:

1. Be very sensitive to human feelings, *tongrenqing* (a word which Japanese informants agreed was best translated as *omoiyari*, i.e., realizing the inner needs of another and responding to them in a non-verbal manner).

2. Be true to the spoken word, *xin*, i.e., do what you promised to do, even if you think that the other person doesn't mind.

3. Develop good *guanxi*, or a network of relationships, by true feelings of friendship, rather than for personal convenience or profit.

4. Once you have made a friend, the rules of *yi*, reciprocal obligation, apply. When you have developed *yi* relationships with somebody, he will treat you like a brother, or member of his family.

5. Family relationships, i.e., *xiao* take precedence over everything else, including *yi* networks of *guanxi* relationships, and written contracts or, equally, verbal agreements.

6. Never express anger, impatience, or disrespect in public. Bad feelings engendered by public criticism, or impoliteness are never forgotten.

7. Indirect ways for correcting errors or showing disagreement are best. E.g., praise a good teacher/student for a job well done, to instruct others how to make changes or correct mistakes.

8. Foreign students who live in Chinese dorms, or with Chinese families, are expected to behave the same as Chinese students, or family members.

9. Never show affection in public, whether to a spouse, fiancé, or girl friend. Asians are very offended to see foreigners over-affectionate with Asian women in public.

10. Chinese are especially sensitive about foreign relationships, due to the past 200 years of colonial and imperialist aggression in China. England, Japan, and Russia are the worst offenders, but all foreigners, American, French, Spanish, etc., appear to be insensitive, even barbaric in their manners towards Chinese and other Asians.

11. Never praise one's nation while putting down or despising (*kanbuqi*) China. There are many things obviously wrong in modern China, but find good things to say as well.

12. Han Chinese find it very hard to forgive an offense. The Opium War, the Boxer Rebellion, extraterritoriality, the war with Japan, American criticism of China, are still fresh memories for all Han Chinese.

13. It is best not to debate or be critical about politics at any time, while living as foreigners in China. If you hear Chinese criticizing the government, listen, but do not express your own feelings about China's leaders publicly. Do not write or say anything that you would not want to be seen on the front page of the morning paper. Everything you do or say becomes public knowledge in the Chinese community you live in.

14. The person of true refinement always makes excuses for failures and lack of courtesy shown by others, as when buying in stores, driving in heavy traffic, or showing intellectual disagreement.

15. When disagreeing with someone else's opinion, or suggesting a correction in a written essay, one could say, for instance, "I would like to brush a few specks of dust off a marvelous piece of polished jade," or some such refined politeness.

16. Respect is shown by putting others up, rather than down. Remember the saying of Lao-tzu: "The reason the ocean is the greatest

of all things is because it is the lowest. Therefore everything flows into its embrace."

17. Thrift, the Chinese word *jiejian*, is a value not understood by foreigners. Any display of wealth, or ostentation is distasteful to a person of refinement and education. Take the bus, rather than a taxi, dress modestly, do not show off affluence. Money displayed will soon be borrowed.

18. *Li*, or polite respect, is the basic underlying value of Chinese society. To take joy in the human encounter, and treat others with deference, opens all doors in China.

This list of behavioral values and sensitivity issues was given to me after my first lecture on the TAT responses. It proved to be extremely valuable, both as a classroom teaching device, and as an aid for conducting my later family studies. I distribute this list to my students at the beginning of each semester, and have received hundreds of pages of response in return. There have been no basic disagreements expressed with the contents of the document, but many more particular pieces of advice given to me instead. *Li shang wai lai*, (respect is the basis for all relationships) is frequently added. *Xiao*, love and respect for members of one's family, and *zhong* or loyalty to the sovereignty and cultural heritage of China, occurred very frequently in the responses of informants in Beijing, who were overwhelmingly in accord with the 1962 list of cultural values (i.e., in 1998, thirty six years after its formulation).

An unspoken value of all the Chinese respondents to my interviews was the fact that they have eternal tenure within their family, and can always rely on parents, siblings, or even close relatives for assistance when needed. This fact was true for adopted children as well as uterine members of the family. The ties binding to family, *by birth or adoption*, last for an entire lifetime.

Yi, or family like reciprocal obligations are clearly generated by *guanxi* relationships existing between friends, as well as between people from the same *xiang* rural area or township in China. This relationship is what Fei Xiaotong has called *chaxugeju*, termed "The differential mode of association" in Gary G. Hamilton and Wang Zheng's sensitive translation of Fei's classic *Xiangtu Zhongguo* ("From the Soil," the

Foundations of Chinese Society, Berkeley: 1992, ch. 5, pp. 60-70). In this sense, Chinese society, Fei writes, can be seen as "webs woven out of countless personal relationships." (ibid., p. 78). Fei further states that the use of native place relationships is "the projection of consanguinity into space'" (introduction, p. 31, quoting Ch. 12, p. 123). In this sense, the creation of *guanxi* or *yi* alliances makes those business people who enter into such relationships "like consanguine relatives" in the conducting of mutually beneficial transactions. Family values become the basis for business ventures and friendship associations, acting as cognate rules for interpersonal relationships in the multli-layered levels of social life.

Perhaps the most important conclusion to be drawn from this lengthy study, which has lasted almost half a lifetime, is the emotional stability, vitality, and security manifested by so many members of the Chinese families who were my hosts and informants. To sit at table during breakfast, lunch, and dinner is a lesson in the joy of indulging and scolding children, and looking after aging grandparents.

Watching Shandong grandmother boil millet and corn gruel, fry left over *jiaozi (chiao-tzu)* to be eaten with steamed bread in the morning, for the family of the daughter whom she once adopted out, says something for the strength of the north China peasant who has survived wars, famines, and floods without any diminished sense of worth and value for the self, or the strong ties of household lineage. If nothing else, the velvet bonds of family bring a security unmatched by any academic or business tenure in the world I return to, as this work is finished, and I send it off to final gestation, where it can no longer be added to by the wealth of details and stories supplied to me by the families who enliven these pages.

APPENDIX

1) *The Five Economic Clasees*

This appendix presents a catalogue of the five socio-economic statuses, and the occupations found in each, based on lists of occupations compiled by the Japanese, tax records, and local Chinese gazetteers. (Nb., the occupations are listed as found in the registers).

Grade 1. High class (named in Local Gazeteers)

A.L. (absentee landlord), banker, M.D., scholar (in a private school) or member of a poetry reading club, lawyer, head of a government run corporation, high ranking civil service/ white collar post such as ward master, city or county council member, CPA.

Grade 2a. Wealthy business owners, entrepreneurs

Business entrepreneur, general supply store owner (GSS) pharmacy (including opium dealer), confectionery, rice merchant, meat, fish, printing, transportation, dry goods, lumber, hats, china, clothes, cement, fabric dying, fertilizer, coal, charcoal (owner), loans/banker, building contractor, restaurant owners, jeweler, renter of apartments (landlord), paper goods, stationery, paper mill, high tax payers.

Grade 2b. Merchant class

Meat sellers, clerks, shop owners, other clerks (bank, rice growers union, credit union), police officers, bakeries.

Grade 2c. Artisan class, some learning, (light labor)

Craftsman, artisan, carpenter, plasterer, silvercraft, stone mason, coffin maker, furniture maker, carpenter, confectionery maker, tailor, fabric dyer, tatami maker, bucket maker, blacksmith, cobbler (make and repair shoes), bamboo crafts, lantern maker, wreath maker (funeral), noodle maker (mifun), tofu, soy-sauce, wine, cook, animal slaughterer, low civil servant, P.O. clerk, mail delivery, police department employee, town office clerk, tax office clerk, telephone operator, railway worker, fire department, bureau of epidemics employee, prison guard, barrier, clergy (Taoist, geomancer, fortune teller). (N.b., Buddhists were not registered under a household).

Grade 3. Heavy physical labor, low status

Manual laborer, coolie, day worker, laundry, seamstress, barber, rickshaw puller, ox-cart, janitor, porter, paper hat weaver, hat maker, peddler, actor, puppet show, musician, pig castration operator, courtesan, temple keeper.

Even though grades 2c and 3 are often not economically different, higher or lower status is given according to the values of the traditional Chinese social system. Though the daily wages are not different for a coolie, brick-layer, or shoe maker, social status is nevertheless higher for the 2c status, as can be seen from the marriage patterns. Social-economic status is measured by leisure and literacy, as well as wealth.

2) *Difference between "O" (related) and "A" (non-related) categories*

    a) The "O" category: blood related.

      1. Son or daughter of the household head

      2. Nephew or niece of the household head, cousin,

    uncle, aunt, blood relative to the sixth degree.

    b) The "A" category: non blood related, different surname.

      3. "Adopted" regardless of relation to household head.

      4. Illegitimate or concubine born.

      5. Household head with no father existing at the

    time of marriage.

      6. Lodger (male/female) with different surname,

    female bond-servant.

      7. Formerly married

3) *Classification of the Chinese Family according to Size*

    a) Nucear family (*jia*), mother, father, children.

    b) Uterine family, bond between mother and children.

    c) Extended family (*fang*), same surname, living behind the same doorway, as different households.

    d) Grand family (*zu*), three generations, grandparents, parents, and children living as a single household.

4) *Sifa (Szu-fa), Customary law and the Chinese Family*

    The term *sifa* (*szu-fa*) is used in the Chinese legal system as a way of codifying local customs. *Tongyangxi* (*t'ung-yang hsi*) child bride, concubine relationships, all forms of adoption and the buying of servants or *yatou* slaves, are classified as *sifa*, local customary law.

134

SELECT BIBLIOGRAPHY

The books listed here represent standard studies on the family in Taiwan, mainland China, and the discussions between Arthur Wolf and Maurice Freedman on the nature of the Chinese family. The books and sources used in *Velvet Bonds* are found in the text and end notes.

Ahern, Emily, *The Cult of the Dead in a Chinese Village*, Stanford: 1973

Baker, Hugh, *A Chinese Lineage Village*, Stanford: 1968

Cohen, Myron, *House United, House Divided*, New York: 1976

Fei Xiaotong, *Peasant Life in China*, New York: 1939

Freedman, Maurice, *Family & Kinship in Chinese Society*, Stanford: 1970

_____, *The Study of Chinese Society*, Stanford: 1979

_____, *Lineage Organization in ES China*, London: 1958

_____, *Chinese Lineage and Society*, London, 1966

Gallin, Bernard, *Hsing Hsing Village, Taiwan: A Chinese Village in Change*, Berkely: 1966

Gamble, Sydney, *Ting Hsien, A North China Rural Community*, New York: 1954

Hsu, Francis, *Under the Ancestor's Shadow*, New York: 1971

Kulp, Danial, *Country Life in South China*, New York: 1925

Lang, Olga, *Chinese Family and Society*, New Haven: 1946

Osgood, Cornelius, *Village Life in Old China*, New York, 1963

Pasternak, Burton, *Kinship and Community in Two Chinese Villages,* Stanford: 1972

Potter, Jack, *Capitalism and the Chinese Peasant: Social and Economic Change in a Hongkong Village*, Berkely: 1969

Purcell, Victor, *The Chinese in Southeast Asia*, London: 1965

Skinner, George William, *Chinese Society in Thailand: An Analytical History*, Ithaca, New York: 1957

Watson, Rubie & Ebrey, Patricia, *Marriage and Inequality in Chinese Society*, Berkely: 1991

Wolf, Arthur (edit.), *Studies in Chinese Society*, Stanford: 1978

Wolf, Arthur & Huang Chieh-shan, *Marriage and Adoption in China*, Stanford: 1980 (extensive bibliography)

Wolf, Margery, *The House of Lim*, New York: 1968

_____, *Women and the Family in Rural Taiwan*, Stanford: 1972

Wolf, Margery & Witke, Roxanne (edit.), *Women in Chinese Society*, Stanford, 1974 (1990)

Yang, Martin, *A Chinese Village: Taitou, Shantong*, New York: 1945

GLOSSARY OF CHINESE TERMS

chao-hsu 招婿 — zhaoxu, uxorilocal husband

chao-fu 招夫 — zhaofu, widow-called in husband

chao-ju 招入 — zhaoru, FHH called in husband

ch'in-ch'i 亲戚 — qinqi, relative

fen-chia 分家 — fenjia, to divide the inheritance

hsiao 孝 — xiao, filiality, love of parents

hsiao-nu 孝女 — 'Filial daughter' (prostitute)

hu-chi 戶籍 — huji, household register

chieh-chien 节减 — jiejian, frugality

kuo-chia 國家 — guojia, the nation family

kuo-fang-zi 过房子 — same surname adoption, boy

li 礼 禮 — respect

li-hun 離婚 — divorce

li-yuan 離願 — break an engagement or adoption

ming-ling-tzu 螟蛉子 — adopted boy of different surname

jen 仁 — ren, benevolence (*bene volens*)

simpua 媳夫阿 — xifu-a, child adopted to be a bride

t'ung-yang-hsi 同養媳 — tongyangxi, same as a simpua

waidiren 外地人 — outsider, from a distant province

yang-nu 養女 — adopted girl

yi 義 — reciprocity, duty

137

INDEX OF SPECIAL TERMS

kinds of marriage, and socio-
economic status, 112
- and relation to HH, 120
kinship, computation of, 81
koseki (see *hu-chi*), 78, ff.
kuo-chia (guojia), a family
kingdom, 5
kuo-fang-tzu, same surname
adoption, 16, 86

landlord family, 21-26
li, respect, xii, 5, 131
li-hun, divorce 16
li-yuan, breaking off adoption
or engagement, 16

marriage, kinds of, 82, q.v.,
- Major, (M) between
adults,
- minor, (m) with a girl
adopted as a child or mini-
bride to marry a boy of the
family, 28, 85
- uxorilocal, children take
the name of the bride's
family, 84
- concubine, recognizing
paternity, 86
- socio-economic status &,
112, 115
- relation to household
head (HH) 120, 121
ming-ling-tzu, a boy adopted
froma family with a different surname, 83
- adopted to marry a
simpua, 88-89
minor marriage stats., 104-05
Muosuo matriarchy, 57-67

Odes, Book of, & courtship,
family-village values, 8

"O" category (blood relation)
93, 134

Police family, 40-42
proportion of M, m, and U
marriages, 101-102

ren (jen) benevolence,
"wishing well" to others,
fellow villager, stranger, 5

Shandong family in Beijing,
33-40
simpua girl adopted to be
married to a son of the
family, 16, 79, 87-89
(See also *t'ung-yang hsi*)
- keeps her family name, 81
- six reasons for, 87-89
- proportion of, 101
- bought and given, 107
- pregnant before marriage,
121

TAT (thematic apperceptive
tests) 124-127
tung-yang-hsi (tongyangxi)
see *simpua*, above.
Tibetan family in Amdo, 50-
53

uterine family, 134
uxorilocal marriage, see *chao-
hsü* above. Husband who
marries into the wife's
family, so that the wife's
family name will continue.

values, Chinese family and
society, identified, 129-131

140

waidiren, people from
  outside Beijing, an
  "outsider," 43-46
woman HH (household head)
  80-81

xiao (hsiao), filiality, parent-
  child and child-parent
  relationship; the basic
  value of the Chinese family, xii, 5, 131
Xia, ancient kingdom whose
  rulers portrayed traditional
  Chinese family values, 1

yang-nü, adopted girl, as
  daughter, 16, 86
- becomes FHH, 18

Yao, Shun, and Yu, ancient
  rulers who typified social
  values, 1
ya-t'ou, a slave girl, 16; see
  ca-bo-gan
yi, reciprocity; duty, in business, friendship 5, 131
yin-chü, retired HH, 82
yin-yang five elements, 6, ff.

za-bo-gan, slave girl, Minnan
  dialect, spelled *ca-bo-gan,*
  28; in Chinese family, 74-79